BARBARISM WITH A HUMAN FACE

Bernard-Henri Lévy

BARBARISM

WITH
A HUMAN FACE

TRANSLATED FROM THE FRENCH BY George Holoch

HARPER & ROW, PUBLISHERS

NEW YORK, HAGERSTOWN

SAN FRANCISCO

LONDON

BARBARISM WITH A HUMAN FACE. English translation copyright © 1979 by Harper & Row, Publishers, Inc. All rights reserved. Printed in the United States of America. No part of this book may be used or reproduced in any manner whatsoever without written permission except in the case of brief quotations embodied in critical articles and reviews: For information address Harper & Row, Publishers Inc., 10 East 53rd Street, New York, N.Y. 10022. Published simultaneously in Canada by Fitzhenry & Whiteside Limited, Toronto.

FIRST EDITION

Designed by Sidney Feinberg

Library of Congress Cataloging in Publication Data

Lévy, Bernard Henri.
Barbarism with a human face.

Translation of La barbarie à visage humain.
Includes index.
1. Socialism—History.   2. Power (Social sciences)
3. Totalitarianism.   I. Title.
HX36.L4413   335′.009   78-19822
ISBN 0-06-012597-7

79 80 81 82 10 9 8 7 6 5 4 3 2 1

A Sylvie, depuis six cents ans

A Justine-Juliette, ce roman d'aventure

Contents

Foreword

I am the bastard child of an unholy union between fascism and Stalinism. I am the contemporary of a strange twilight when the clouds above are dissolving amid the clash of arms and the cries of the tortured. The only revolution I know, the one which may grant notoriety to this century, is the Nazi plague and red fascism. Hitler did not die in Berlin. Conqueror of his conquerors, he won the war in the stormy night into which he plunged Europe. Stalin did not die in Moscow nor at the Twentieth Congress. He is here among us, a stowaway in the history that he still haunts and bends to his mad will. You say the world is doing well? It's certain in any case that it keeps on going, since it isn't changing. But never before has the will to death been so nakedly and cynically unleashed. For the first time the gods have left us, no doubt weary of wandering on the plain of ashes where we have made our home. And I am writing in an age of barbarism which is already, silently, remaking the world of men.

If I were a poet, I would sing of the horror of living and

the new Gulags that tomorrow holds in store for us. If I were a musician, I would speak of the idiot laughter and impotent tears, the dreadful uproar made by the lost, camped in the ruins, awaiting their fate. If I had been a painter (a Courbet rather than a David), I would have represented the dust-colored sky lowering over Santiago, Luanda, or Kolyma. But I am neither painter, nor musician, nor poet. I am a philosopher, one who uses ideas and words—words already crushed and macerated by fools. So, with the words of my language, I will do no more than speak of the massacres, the camps, and the processions of death, the ones I have seen and the others, which I also wish to recall. I will be satisfied if I can explain the new totalitarianism of the smiling Princes, who sometimes even promise happiness to their people. This essay should thus be read as an "archaeology of the present," carefully retracing through the fog of contemporary speech and practice the outline and the stamp of a barbarism with a human face.

I will soon be thirty and I have betrayed the dream of my youth at least a hundred times. Like everyone else, I believed in a new and joyful "liberation"; now, without bitterness, I live with the shadows of my past hopes. I believed in revolution, a faith that came from books, no doubt, but all the same I believed in it as a good, the only one that counted and was worth hoping for. Now, feeling the ground give way and the future disintegrate, I wonder not if it is possible but if it is even desirable. I wished to and sometimes did get involved in politics, howling with the wolves and singing in the chorus. I can do so no longer, and I feel like a gambler who has lost hope of winning or like a soldier who no longer believes in the war he is waging. I even believed in happiness, and I love sensuality above all, sensuality that you neither pursue nor beg for, like a blessed respite in the parenthesis that is life. But anguish is stronger and there is no way out of the unholy despair in which men grow fat. "Happy," they say. What do they mean by that?

If I were an antiques dealer, I would like to be able to stuff the glorious remains, the emaciated carcasses that were and still are enthroned in the heaven of optimism. If I were an encyclopedist, I would dream of writing in a dictionary of the year 2000: "Socialism, *n.*, cultural style, born in Paris in 1848, died in Paris in 1968." If I were a surrealist, I would wish to say, like Aragon, that I am, we are the new defeatists of Europe, surrounded by crumbling monuments and newly dug graves which we violate once a year, out of habit. But I am obviously neither a surrealist, nor an encyclopedist, nor an antiques dealer. I am only an "intellectual" who has decided to speak his mind to the experts of progressive thought; a shamelessly irresponsible person who will not easily tire of hunting down philistines and impostors; and especially a pitiful politician who believes in the impossible and in radical evil, but who sticks with the simple thesis that the intolerable also exists, and that we must resist it with every breath. Am I a *moraliste?* Why not? I have attempted nothing in this book but to think through to the end the idea of pessimism in history.

As the tenant of my name and a journeyman of passing time, I have no claim to write except as a witness. Since I am absent from the making of history and have been formed into the little bit of humanity that I am, I know that I have no right to preach and to prophesy. And yet I have decided to write because I have a passion to persuade. Even so, certain things should be made clear. To my sorrow, I am addressing the left here, the institutionalized left; my target is the left in its passion for delusion and ignorance. I am thinking of those socialists who, in these times of armed vigilance and politicians' fantasies, have the courage and the dignity to call themselves "beautiful souls" and to hold high the torch of lucidity. I write for them, for they are the sentinels of a world that would be worse without them. I am thinking of those political men who know, more and more each day, that the course of events is indecipherable, and who are wise enough to think within the form of history without believing that it has a definite purpose. They are the ones I want to disturb, or at least to question, for they will soon have our fate in their hands.

And then there are the others, the shadows hovering at the edges, the familiar ghosts who have not left me through all the time I was writing, the godparents and protectors I would like to acknowledge at the outset. Christian Jambet and Guy Lardreau, it goes without saying, because were it not for *L'Ange* I probably would not have risked this book. Jean-Marie Benoist, because his joyful irreverence has often kept me alive and adds enchantment to the world. Jean-Paul Dollé, pessimist philosopher, whose bitter rage for thinking has more than once placed me in his debt. Gilles Hertzog, friend, companion, who quite simply knows the meaning of grandeur. Finally, my father, to whom I owe the essential.

PART ONE

THE SHEPHERD
AND HIS FLOCK

—

Everyone knows the perennial philosophical question: "Why is there being, being rather than nothing?" But there is a new problem which we should perhaps, at the risk of vertigo, make it our obligation to deal with: "Why is there power, power rather than nothing?" This question will recur stubbornly and obsessively throughout the pages of this book. This is where I have chosen to begin, with no further preliminaries.

Why power, and how is it contrived? Are there societies without power, and does that notion even have any meaning? How is it that it is permanent, that it changes hands but does not disappear? In other words, what is it that rivets it to men's bodies and fixes it in the heaven of our mental landscape? It is meaningless to philosophize outside that domain. Philosophy would not be worth a moment's effort if it did not first of all take on the form and features of politics.

I imagine that what I have to say will not be fashion-

able, because I am attacking frivolous thinkers and cheerful scoundrels. "Progressives" won't agree either, because they and their impenitent optimism will be called into question. No, the world is not in a good state and it will probably get no better. Yes, the Prince is an inevitability who bends history to his will. Life is a lost cause, and happiness an outmoded idea.

1   The Litany of the Left

What does the traditional left have to say about all this—
I mean the left that recognizes that the spirit of the age
is Marxist? And what is the answer of the new extreme
left, which has taken the idea of liberation as its banner?
In a profound sense they are saying the same thing, using
the same fabric of platitudes, the same stock of commonplaces. This is what the lost souls of the present are living
on.

The left, then. It is settled on a bed of certainties ce-
mented by a century of dogmatism. It has a theory of
power, an authentic and coherent theory, which can, I
think, be summarized in a few key propositions. Men are
dominated, it explains, because they are "manipulated,"
and the tool of this manipulation is called an "ideology."
Ideology is a "lie" instilled in men's minds which forces
them to become "blinded" to the reality of their oppression. This lie works and we resign ourselves to its violence
because of the "ruse" of the Princes who force us to internalize it. And yet we can foil this ruse if only we "unveil"

it and exorcise the spell that held our souls in thrall. The whole Marxist theory of power is there, in that simple and well-knit outline. Any kind of optimism, any belief in a better world, necessarily adopts it as its political charter.

Reread the charter and consider all its unstated assumptions. You will find that it leads to three still simpler and interrelated definitions. In this perspective, the oppressor is a lucid and diabolical anticonfessor, a master of his techniques who governs a population of sleepwalkers. The oppressed is therefore a kind of waking dreamer, a docile and unconscious participant in his own subjection, an involuntary maker of the tools of his unhappiness. And by the same token the rebel becomes a master of the truth, all-powerful because he is wise, and free because he knows he is in chains. All-powerful knowledge, ignorant belief, the Master's perversity . . . Power has everything it needs to survive, but also carries the seeds of its own destruction. It is a matter of science: the wicked science of some, the divine science of others. If you dissipate the illusion, you demystify its attractions.

Read it again, and you will see that the argument is a fraud. On the one hand, it pretends to take the secret springs of power seriously; it adds the weight of history to them to explain their permanence; it methodically enumerates the most minute channels through which the law circulates and the illusion is internalized. But on the other hand, it attempts to minimize the terror it has caused: the mechanisms of power and the institutions of the State mysteriously dissolve under the weight of the forces of knowledge; and all the subtle enumerations and sophisticated analyses finally come to rest in the most banal of Enlightenment theories, in a soft and warm complacency

with a whiff of radicalism: power is a substance that im-
prisons and terrorizes, but it is also a paper tiger creating
more fear than harm. Know and progress, persevere in
optimism, and no Bastille will dare to resist you.

Like all frauds, this one hardly stands up now to the only
meaningful test: concrete history and its cruellest lessons.
How do the Marxists explain, for example, that Europe
before '39 knew for a certainty that Hitler was the name
of an imminent worldwide disaster; that the organizations
of the German left foresaw, if not the extent, at least the
probability of the holocaust; and yet that no one succeeded in halting his progress? How do they explain that
even now, their proletariat, conscientiously educated in
the mysteries of exploitation, the proletariat to whom
they have explained the ruses of capital, has come so easily to terms with those ruses and postponed indefinitely
the moment of outwitting them? How do they explain
that the peoples of the world, in spite of knowing their
true interests, generally take such malicious pleasure in
refusing to recognize the urgency and necessity of bringing them to fruition? An informed slave is never anything
but a happy slave. Informing him of his misfortune always
amounts to liberating him while he is still in chains. There
is a whiff of stoicism behind Marxist optimism, a *knowing*
resignation to the inevitability of an unhappy existence.
There is a strange and colossal abdication on the left, in
the face of the reality of submission.

All this is well known, and I will not dwell on it. But it
is less well known that since '68 there has been a new
wave on the left who think they have overcome the old
blindness, but have in reality repeated essentially the

same process. We know them well, these happy warriors, apostles of drift and celebrators of diversity, anti-Marxist in the extreme and joyful iconoclasts. These dancers of the latest fashion are coming, they're already here, painted and spangled with a thousand flames of unleashed desire, champions of immediate "liberation." These sailors of the modern ship of fools have their helmsmen, Saint Gilles and Saint Félix, shepherds of the flock and authors of *Anti-Oedipus.* Power, they assure us, holds no secrets for them. They have finally found the philosopher's stone; it was just a matter of using Reich to interpret the materialist libido. They have understood that servitude is inevitably tied, welded to man's very being. Men are willing slaves. Hitler succeeded because that's what the German masses desired. They are appropriately called "desirers," because wherever the classic left thinks in terms of institutions, structures, and authorities, they see a subtle and perverse microphysics made up of flux, desire, and pleasure.

At first glance everything distinguishes these Copernicuses of the realm of politics. They have broken their moorings and set out for the open sea. But here again, read carefully and listen. For here, too, everything hinges on a few simple propositions whose very formulation proves that they are essentially the inverse of the others. Men are dominated, they say, not because they are manipulated, but on the contrary because they *wish* it, and at the heart of this wish there is *pleasure* and only pleasure. This pleasure is not a lie imposed on its victims, but the simple truth of their most hidden *impulses*—the "servile intensities" of Jean-François Lyotard. These fantasies persist as an effect not of deception but literally of *love:* the love of the subject for his sovereign and of the oppressed for his misfortune. And we can hope to free ourselves from them by means not of the truth but of *desire* yet again—repressed, inverted, or parasitic desire. All modern leftism is contained in this pattern of thought, as is that of Marxism, with this difference: Where one speaks of "truth," the other speaks of "libido."

This is all the more obvious when the argument is clearly and articulately formulated. It breaks down into three simple definitions, which repeat in distorted form the old optimistic triad. In this new perspective, what is the oppressor? This time, it is he who appears as the waking dreamer, the involuntary object of the enigmatic love of the people, the docile and unconscious idol of a cult he has not really created. The oppressed in turn lucidly and diabolically govern their own unconsciousness, loving with an active love a somehow somnolent Prince. And by the same token the rebel becomes a master not of knowledge but of desire, omnipotent because he is liberated, and liberated because he desires while still in chains. The omnipotence of desire, the extreme will to believe, the relative innocence of the Master: Here, too, power is easily glossed over as it becomes entrenched. It is a matter of assent and the simple will to serve. If you reverse your will and refuse your assent, power collapses at one stroke like a punctured balloon.

Does the parallel seem strained? Look again at the trickery behind the position. On the one hand, its pessimistic side claims to give a complete account of the phenomenon in its darkest and most radical aspects; it directly confronts the riddle of *consciously* accepted submission; it mobilizes all the resources of subtlety to explain the cohesiveness of power, that strange, occult quality which penetrates the social fabric in spite of men's sighs and protests. On the other, it has a radiant, luminous side, in which we see servitude suddenly dissolved by the force of flowing and mysteriously cleansing desire, and power at one stroke seems to become a flabby and empty form, a dead branch fallen from the great tree of life. All the rebel has to do is trumpet his schizophrenia and the walls of the fortress come tumbling down. There are two impulses, two temptations behind this mode of "liberated" thought—a compound of minute attention to detail and carefree improvisation. There is no contradiction; or if there is, it is the same one that undermined Marxian thought.

It is not at all surprising, then, that this leftism, too, stumbles against reality and concrete history. The ruled, we are told, "desire" their rulers. But consider Bataille's argument that the bourgeoisie is the first Western master who no longer knows how to "expend" and therefore no longer fascinates. The proletariat enjoys its "servile intensities"? Deleuze's epigones ought to take a look at industrial barbarism, at the cold and weary hatred that chokes the oppressed at the very moment of their surrender. Germany wanted, desired Hitler with a perverse but authentic and determined desire? This is abject as well as fraudulent; it overlooks *material* interests, men's tangible suffering: the pain of unemployment, for example, and inflation and poverty, which did just as much as the libidinal economy of the time to pave the way for totalitarianism.[1] And to say that liberation has desire as its mainspring, a desire that has been naturalized, released, or decoded, amounts to understanding nothing about the workings of capital, adhering to a kind of "naturalism"[2] which they discredited long ago, and which I myself will attempt to deconstruct. So we have the same examples and parallel blunders, the same images of power, and equally fraudulent interpretations.

We could multiply examples, choose less classic, more sophisticated ones. We could vary the levels of analysis and enter into detail about theoretical mechanisms. But I will stop here for the moment, with these few remarks and this rapid overview. For the basic point has been made, and I draw from it the following conclusions: *Deleuze and Guattari are Marxist philosophers* whose rhetoric follows the materialist model; the new extreme left is no better equipped than the old to understand the essence of power; maintaining the contrary of the old left's mistake, it only asserts a parallel mistake and has nothing to say about the domain of politics that the dialectic has not already said. As a result, we must change ground and find new tools and methods of analysis. We must break off the confrontation between banal Leninism and its leftist double. Power exists, here, unthinkable; and yet we must attempt to think it.

It is important to recognize the degree of this change of ground and the risks it involves. We have to challenge a number of received ideas in order to escape from the leftists' dead ends. In the last analysis, everything is staked on two basic ideas that form the skeleton of every variety of political optimism, ideas so basic that it is hard to see how to get around them and on what grounds they can be criticized. First, the Master is not unreal; he is a visible and concrete being enjoying all the benefits of ontological existence. A power that deceives and manipulates or an object that calls forth and provokes desire; a state that exploits or oppresses or a lovable and beloved Prince; in every case we are dealing with a *reality* whose words have the weight of things, a reality securely established in the economy of the world. We may describe this reality in terms of the mechanisms of power or of desire, as a hegemony imposed from without or called for from within, as an authority crowning the social structure or as a microphysical phenomenon dispersed on its surface; in every case we are only providing theoretical clothes for our most immediate and irresistible conviction. We are only confirming what everyone knows or thinks he knows: The Master is the name of a thing, that thing has a basis, and that thing and its basis can and must be *localized*. In other words, power is neither a word nor an image, and there is nothing illusory or fantastical about it. It has an authentic substance; better, it is that very substance or its foundation.

The second idea is a corollary of the first. *The Master, who is not unreal, is nevertheless almost unreal.* Seen from a different angle, his ontological weight is not as great as we thought; he can suddenly tumble into the realm of the invisible and the darkness of abstraction. Manipulation fails, desire withdraws, a fragile state enters into crisis, a Prince is demystified: The Master can suddenly sink into the nothingness of anarchy, become as light as the wave or the crisis that destroys him, vacate the material space where he was enthroned in majesty. Leninists speak of "revolution" and "awakening consciousness," leftists of "liberation" or abstention from "desire." Leninists speak of "struggle" and "strategy," leftists of a "transversal break," but they are all only giving philo-

sophical form to the most ineradicable belief of the oppressed. At the deepest level, they are doing nothing but
restating in their way what everyone believes or wants to
believe: The Master is not everything he claims to be,
and we can desire or assert his essential vulnerability. It
doesn't matter that he's not made out of thin air; he can
be dissolved, unmade. Even though he is the monument
he wishes to be, he is threatened by ruin and collapse. In
spite of all his armor, like everything else he is mortal.

This is the militants' faith, then, following after the wisdom of the ages, the realm of hope after the realm of
fatalism. What could be more irrefutable than this double
stupefaction? How can we dare to deny the glaring evidence of the facts? Above all, who can contradict the
melancholy assurance of faith? Our impostors cooperate
in establishing an article of belief, and this article of belief
seems impregnable as long as it is armed with common
sense. And yet we must go against what "goes without
saying" and once more begin to think.

2   The Prince is Another Name for the World

Things are clear now, and our path is clearly set out. But our backs are to the wall and our heads almost empty. One thing and only one thing is certain: We have to answer these leftist litanies point by point.

Power is not nothing? Our answer must be, whatever the cost, that that is granting it too much and, in a sense, overestimating it. We must counter the "desirers" by saying that the Prince has no obvious attribute that would make him able to captivate desire, and counter the Marxists by saying that he possesses no distinction that would give rise to the violence of his rule. We must answer both groups that he is neither man nor thing, but a *nothing* without foundation, without a determinate place of his own. Carried to its conclusion, this means concretely that if there are in the world something like effects of power, visible and precise effects physically experienced by men, they are effects of an absent cause and perhaps without any cause at all, primary and underived effects and therefore self-creating. Or else, if supporters and agents of power do exist—Princes, for example, or particular states —the idea of a ruling class is meaningless, and so is the idea of an *ideology* contaminating the social fabric from its stronghold. Finally, we can say this: If we get rid of all the classic images, the notions of "quiddity" and substantiality which persist in granting him ontological weight, we must bring ourselves to distinguish the master of this world, who has a flesh-and-blood existence, from the Master in general, who is enthroned nowhere. *These are three ways of saying that power in its essence is in no way material, that it has no essence at all in a philosophical sense, that it is an apparently unnamable figment of the imagination.*

In turn, there is only one way of thinking about this figment of the imagination. Power has always been defined as a principle springing from a source and flowing into its branches. It must be defined in the opposite way, as an effect that comes from below, returns from the periphery, and rises from the depths of the world. It has always been described as though it were a plague, a strange disease attacking a healthy body, spreading terror and corrupting innocence. We have to reverse the metaphor and describe it as a returning tide, the smell of a diseased body which has been corrupted from the very beginning and terrorized from within. It has always been said that the ruled *internalize* violence, *identify* with the Prince, and *swallow* his orders. Why not, on the contrary, imagine a *hemorrhage,* an *expulsion* of the Prince, and an *externalization* of the law? Concretely, this in turn would imply that there is no domination, that oppression does not exist, that we are oppressed without oppressors to rule over us. The Prince is not a ruler perched in a watchtower or ensconced in a desire factory, but an "ego ideal" set up by the individual and projected into an ideal heaven. The cop isn't in our heads, he hasn't been there for a long time, because we have expelled him precisely in order to sublimate him and give him concrete form.

Power is almost nothing, says the leftist litany. Here, too, we have to grasp the paradox firmly and refrain from accepting the assurances of optimism. *Resist* evil? If domination is nothing, if it has no basis, no resistance against it is possible. *Liberate* ourselves from destiny? Power has no location, because it is the Ground of all grounds, and there is no ground in nature on which a good nature might stand. *Dethrone* the Prince? If the Prince has no throne and no definite place, he can never be reached and we can never attack the kernel of his authority. Concretely, this means that if we have just granted him too much, now we are granting him too little; if we overestimated his ontological weight, now we are underestimating his power; and perhaps precisely because he is not *one* thing, because he is a *nothing,* he thereby becomes *all,* all of reality and the entire world. Even more concretely, if domination's only basis is submission, strictly speaking submission has no more reality than domination. If there are no "rulers" confronting the "ruled," perhaps the ruled have no more existence than the rulers. If authority has no roots, no location, and no density, then revolt cannot be radical, and there is no way it can come into existence. Even though, as I have said, slaves create their masters and the universe echoes with the millennial rattling of their chains, their revolt, too, is a figment of the imagination in the same sense that power is.

If, on this point, I had to clothe myself with the authority of a great man, if I had to clarify this disturbing dialectic further, I would choose to refer to La Boétie's admirable *Discours de la servitude volontaire*.[3] He was the first
at least to raise the question of "voluntary servitude,"
which has little to do with the banal and abject "desire for
submission" invented by the moderns. What precisely
does he say? That men *produce* their own submission, but
all the same, they neither desire nor enjoy it; in fact, they
desire and love it so little that they never stop protesting
against its yoke. But this revolt is somehow afflicted with
a curse, and always and everywhere transformed into a
new variety of servitude. For mastery is the law of this
world, and no proclamation, no earthquake, can ever succeed in overturning it. What does this mean? In this history, there is no duality of desire, no confrontation of
opposed principles; there is no class struggle that will not
end up with the restoration of peace and unity; no counterpower that is not finally an embodiment of power
renewed; no alternative, no plurality, no dissidence, that
are not quickly reduced to a grimace on the face of
homogeneity. *The Prince is another name for the world.
The Master is a metaphor for reality. There is no ontology
that is not a politics.*

To recapitulate. Against the Deleuzeans, who agree in
their fashion that power is an emanation, a product of the
dominated, but who attribute this emanation to a perverse pleasure in servitude, I have attempted to suggest
the idea of a *collective hemorrhage* of the sort analysts
describe as producing an ego ideal outside the ego.
Against the Marxists, who agree that power is a whole

which can tolerate no counterpower, that the State, for example, is a mechanism which absorbs and annihilates any pockets of nonpower, I have attempted to point to a *Domination* whose absorbing force and annihilating power are the result of something other than violence and ideology. Against both, who make the Prince into a thing among things, to vanish one fine day into the nothingness of liberation, I think we have to make of him, simultaneously, an *unreal image* because he has no precise location, and an *insurmountable totality* because he embraces with a single law the differences and the unities of the world. There are thus three requirements that have to be linked to one another, three principles whose very foundations have to be thought through together. This will probably be the task of a philosophy of the future, which will reject the mirages and illusions of sophistry. It is in any case the task of any thought undertaking a theory of politics, even at the cost of the darkest and most tragic pessimism. It is the central riddle of this essay, which, on this point, aims at nothing less than laying the groundwork for a new theory of power.

I have said enough for now to be able to take one more step and, if not to set out this series of paradoxes in an orderly way, at least to sketch what such an order might be. The idea of the "all and nothing" that is power, of the simple name of Master, which is also the Name of all names, of drifting unreality coupled with prodigious omnipotence, can be found in the work of the Freudians, and only there. In fact, they have a word and a concept to embody this mysterious reality shot through with unreality, this unnamable figure we never stop naming. The concept is perhaps quite simply what they call a "fantasy."

Like power, a fantasy cannot be found; it is impalpable, a pure void created by its tool—literally its creature. It is also an unreality stronger than reality, imposing its law, and forcing its way into reality—in fact, a necessity of reality. It is, finally, the condition of the health and the survival of the one who produces it, the transfigured form of a radical and unfathomable evil, the necessary detour by which we learn to die and to support life—in this sense its redemption. I have used the word "fantasy." Don't expect a treatise on the paucity of reality. You should not imagine that the Master is nothing but a mist of power or think of the "Imaginary" as a delusion and a shadow. For I am saying the opposite, assuming with Lacan that the Imaginary, the domain of this fantasy, is indissolubly linked on the one hand to the realm of the symbolic, where the signifier-Master rules, and on the other to reality—that is, to the lack which comes to animate the infernal circle of desire for beings destined to die and condemned to speak. Like Augustine's trinity, where the Father is never present without the Son and the Holy Ghost, the Imaginary is never present without the two other manifestations. (On this point, see Lacan's latest discussion of the theory of knots.) In this sense, and only in this sense, Freudianism can be seen as a political recourse, a means of escaping from the appearances of "leftist" thought.

For, saying that the Prince is a fantasy of his subjects, an actor in their imaginary theater, grants him *as little as possible* on the level of material existence: He is an authentic nothingness of being, a pure human sigh, a figment of the imagination. At the same time, it grants him *as much weight as possible* on the level of power: He soon becomes reality, their inescapable reality, the enclosed arena in which they have to live and suffer. The Deleuzeans clearly recognize that power is in some sense bound up with human nature, that it is not imposed on men but on the contrary derives from them. But they conceive of the connection in terms of "desire," they see desire itself as energy without purpose or external aim, and they imagine it reversing itself, turning back on itself, or wearing itself out as it wanders on its senseless way. The Freudians also see the bond that ties power to the soul, but their use of the word "fantasy" helps them to understand the permanence, the eternity of the bond, which points not toward confusion but toward the very conditions for the survival of the species. And the bond cannot turn back on itself, reverse itself, or wear itself out without endangering the conditions and the very fact of that survival.

If this is so, must we still persist in speaking of "power"? The allusion to Freud suggests at least one thing. Perhaps "power" means nothing but the "will to live" or the "will to survive."

3 Bonds Are Shackles

That is what remains to be thought through in the dismal ruins of the aftermath of May '68. We have to dare to assert certain things against the holy family of avuncular Marxism and laughing leftism. Power is not, as we have been so insistently taught, the result of class societies and their perverse machinations. Nor is it an unholy alliance in the mind of the oppressed of the Prince's action and the desire for submission. Nor is it that fragile entity a shameful disease, which the preachers of enlightenment would like to cure. There is perhaps—I would say certainly—something in the very existence of societies that condemns them to servitude and misery. Perhaps—doubtless—there is something in the simple act of association that makes the Master necessary, indeed inevitable. And this is what a pessimistic philosophy of today must examine, this disturbing and terrifying riddle.

I know the problem is difficult, and posing the question so harshly leads directly to vertigo in the face of the intolerable and the impossible. At this point, as you may have guessed, what is at stake is the basis of our illusions, the hard core of optimism. And the landmarks are few on this path, past the wretched guard of honor that history provides for happiness. No doubt that's why I suddenly feel tempted to call for help, to gather around me that small band of heralds, the exemplary deserters who, in the solitude of madness, at the threshold of death, their bodies riddled with stars and their faces streaming with tears, send us a sign from afar. Only these disturbing presences have dared to tell the agonizingly comic tale of the "will to live," they alone have been able to speak of the inexhaustible horror of the pure and simple social bond. I am thinking of the philosophers, of course, the melancholy experts in absolute evil, Plato and Schopenhauer. I am thinking of Artaud, Bataille, the outcast surrealists and minor romantics, Jacques Vaché and Pétrus Borel, society's suicides, angels of despair.

And above all there is Rousseau,[4] whom I dare not call my master and whom I invoke with dread, so great was his knowledge of the meaning of suffering. Destitute, defiled, disgusting, he was spurned, slandered, tortured, beaten, and masturbated to death by a century that could not bear to hear him speak of the miasma of its Enlightenment. He proclaimed to the bitter end his hatred of the scornful, the gang of lackeys, cardinals, and cops who make the laws of this world and never tire of singing its praises. Alone against his time, alone against an age of iron, alone against the theodicies of every time and place, he believed it his duty to denounce infamy in the most infamous way, and to give an account of the intolerable in the most intolerable language. He offered a beautiful and gloomy theory of the impossibility of giving a social form to the good and to happiness, and a somber affirmation of the impossibility of peace in the world, a world he would have liked to forget because of all it made him suffer.

It is time to reread the *Second Discourse,* less as an idyllic picture of some original state of nature than as an implacable assault against Condorcet's "Progress," Turgot's "Perfectibility," and the "Freedom" of Voltaire and Diderot—all of them turned into their opposites in the infernal spiral of immemorial servitude. It should be read less as a banal and delicate defense of vital and powerful speech and of the real presence of the self than as a stubborn and insistent elaboration of the intuition that wherever distance, division, and separation exist, there is already the seed of relations based on force and power. It is also time to reread the beginning of *The Social Contract* and to see in it exactly the opposite of what fools see, the opposite of a plan for society, a concrete utopia, or a political vade mecum for the Princes of the time—the Poles one day and Robespierre the next. It is time to understand literally the famous definition of the contractual agreement which "everyone makes *with himself,"* and not *with others,* which does not refer to others and is not a contract for peace and liberality among equals, an alliance of neighbors, but a radical break with the very idea of a social bond.

Most important of all, perhaps, we have to rethink the place of *Émile* in the body of his work, give up seeing it as the traditional treatise on education attached as an appendix to every theory of society, and restore it to the rightfully central position its author assigned to it in a famous letter. From that position he proclaims, once more against the Enlightenment, that there is not, nor can there be, happiness for an institution; and that because it presupposes "comparison," transforms pure "self-love" into "selfishness," and separates man's "being" from his "appearance," the simple relation to others constitutes the evil stage where the chains of subjection are forged. Even so, Rousseau is not Liu Shao-chi, nor is he Montaigne, and he was not the tutor of kings. *Émile* says nothing other than that the idea of a good *society* is an absurd dream, a contradiction in terms, and the idea of *public* welfare, soon to become the Revolutionaries' pork barrel, is an idea of dreamers who quickly turn into assassins.

After two hundred years, we can recognize today the originality of his argument, what distinguishes it from both the pessimism of the right and the optimism of the left, from the problematics of the two sides of natural law. On one hand, power is claimed to be natural and therefore eternal; on the other, it is claimed to be cultural and therefore destructible. Rousseau was the first to say neither the latter, which is a lie, nor the former, which is abject. He escapes from the alternative which leaves a choice only between original evil and promised beatitude. He says, and this is entirely different, that power is eternal and destructible at the same time, eternal as society is and destructible as society is as well. He does not claim that misery will last as long as human nature lasts, but as long as that nature comes together in a social bond. He does not say that tomorrow will be better because history will change and culture will progress, but that tomorrow will be like today as long as there is history and culture. He does not say that salvation is unthinkable, but intuits its dependence on the end of societies, on the end of history that chains us to them, even if that entails provisionally confirming it within the precarious and dreamlike enclosure of a solitary soliloquy. His pessimism, in other words, is no longer the same as the pessimism of Bossuet, preacher of Gallicanism and theoretician of the divine right of kings, who attributed the existence of the Prince to the fragility of man and his "natural iniquity." It is already the pessimism of Hegel, who attributed the existence of the Prince to the undiscoverable event of the birth of history and of humanity as a herd.

I believe this to be a central political thesis of Hegelianism; in any case, one that applies to the present. It is urgent to return to the idea, developed in the *Phenomenology,* of the "objectification of the self," which is always tragically transformed into "alienation"; the idea of a consciousness which comes into contact with the world, expends itself in works, and joins with others, only to be lost in those others, divided in those works, and abolished in that world. The world is never anything but negativity and contradiction, separation and misery, constantly and unreservedly renewed in a dialectical process. We should return to Hegel, then, against Marx the critic of Hegel, against the Marx who maintained that there are "objectifications" that are not "alienations"; that they are distinguishable in theory if not in fact; and that the revolution is precisely the moment of truth that abolishes the root of the confusion and opens up the springs of happiness. If you make the effort to read it from a political perspective, the *Logic* says nothing more than that as long as the world is spirit, its history will be the history of the dialectic—we would say of lordship. As long as the world is the world—that is, social organization—the world and society will presuppose the dispossession of the self, its internal division, and its separation from others—we would simply say power. The professor from Jena was not wrong when he saw in the modern state the culmination of the West. He was not wrong because, to all appearances, the age of the greatest submission is the age of the most powerful and successful socialization.

Besides, this is perfectly clear to the rebels of modern times, to the rebels of all times, those who have gone blind from staring at the horror, who have exhausted their strength and sometimes their will to live in their unending assault against the fortress of lordship. They know perfectly well that rebellion is unthinkable inside the real world; that it is foolish to claim that rebellion can be socialized, because it is a negation of society, of what makes society livable; and that there are no rebels in history who are not first of all *deserters*. They know it, too, in the U.S.S.R., the ones who paid with their lives for their opposition to the Prince of the day, a Prince who knotted the social bonds tighter than ever before. It has been said over and over that there is a strange mystery in the mechanism of the Moscow trials and in the attitudes of their victims; in their silent acceptance of the role they were made to play; in their tacit approval of the principle of their defeat; in the litanies they continued to recite, even as they climbed the scaffold, in praise of the party which "is never mistaken" and against which no one is right. This riddle can be solved only if we understand that they were engaged in a death struggle with existing power and that their defeat could lead only to the loss of their very being, their reality as men, speaking and desiring men, real historical men. Not that torture and terror took it from them by force, but they condemned themselves by the act of opposition to silence and desocialization. Nameless and faceless old Bolsheviks, uncertain of their origins, not caring about their age, they paid for their rebellion with an absolute social death. Like the "beautiful souls" of the *Phenomenology,* they could only dissolve like mist in the air, eradicated from their homes, forever outcast.

They are an extreme case, of course, but they reveal more about power than many learned treatises. Power is not a foreign body in society, but an integral part of it: it is *the founder of social conditions.* We have to stop thinking of it as a parasite or a diadem, an ornament or an insignia; it is *the means by which a society organizes itself,* gives itself the character it chooses, and arranges itself harmoniously. It is a symbol more than an effigy, and it serves less to crown society than to *establish* it. Consider, for example, the modern state and its mode of operation. It reproduces its foundation only by stirring up and reproducing dissidence against its natural linearity; by generating otherness against the inhibitions of singleness; by bringing forth diversity in the field of identity. And then it operates only by making this symbolically established dissidence into a simple form of difference; by molding that otherness into the shape of death and unity; by converting diversity into a rediscovered identity. Power is not a poison, a bacillus eating away at some primeval condition of social health; it is the demiurge without which society and its health would not exist. Nor is it the tool described by the Marxists, devoted to repression and to the maintenance of order in the mechanisms of social conflict. Or rather it is a tool only in the very specific sense that it is used for socialization, for the establishment of society. It is not even a ground of legitimacy in the Weberian sense; legitimacy seems to be given to it beforehand, and its fundamental function is to make the *multitudo dissoluta* into the body of a sovereign and the web of a social bond. What does power do? It is the constant basis for the existence of societies. What is the Prince? He is the way men unite only by dividing themselves from the good.

PART TWO

ALL SORTS AND
CONDITIONS OF MASTER

■

Politicians may protest as loudly as they want, slaves and the oppressed become drunk with wild hopes, and certified optimists tell us their fairy tales: The Master is always right because he is another name for the world. He will not tire of being right as long as society exists. Until now humanity without power has meant barbarism. So there is no debt to be paid off, no claim on fate, no tithe to be collected from misery. Revolution in the true sense is an impossibility.

Having said that, we've hardly gotten any further. Our backs are still to the wall, and our heads barely less empty. Hence the next few chapters, in which I will unfetter and concretize the abstract thesis, set out its consequences in order, and survey the extent of its truth. I will test it to the very end, exploring its most unexpected implications. These chapters should be read, then, as prolegomena to any philosophy taking on the task of looking at evil face to face.

There is no society without power, and no social bond not established by the Master? Very precisely, this means that there is no desire, no language, no reality, and no history free from the dominion of identity. Identity can provide no possible haven for a radical break, nor can it be made into a banner. And it is meaningless to speak of a "desire" for revolution, of a revolutionary "language," of socialist "reality," and of popular or proletarian "history."

4   The Dawn of Law

As for desire, I can do no better than to refer once again to the broad lines of Freudian political theory, as presented, for example, in the excellent book by Pierre Legendre.[1] No one has described more accurately the stock of ancient fantasies that haunt canon law and whose procedures are still endlessly repeated by our technocrats. No one has shown more clearly how the coldest and most disembodied methods of administration draw upon a reservoir of strange Oedipal symbols whose spells could be exorcised only by psychoanalysis. It is particularly important to read his note on the classic distinction between public and private law, nothing but a juridical version of the theme of imaginary castration. His chapter on the language of advertising, those whispered words straight from theocratic theologies, shows how it does nothing but endlessly repeat their ancient sexual messages. This clearly means that every collective psychology presupposes an individual psychology; that the administration of things presupposes the administration of men; that there is no systematic knowledge of humanity and no management of human cattle not based on an anthropology, a science of man and his desires. As a result, politics, as a science and a separate domain, literally does not exist.

Alternatively, another way of saying the same thing, desire does not exist as an autonomous entity; it has no specific, definable place from which the law might lead it astray. It does not antedate power, in the limbo of some mute and nomadic natural world. We have to stop thinking of it as a captive reality, governed from outside and crushed by the law, for it is nothing before its captivity. Crushed from the outset, it has always been scarred and burdened by want. We have to get rid of the tenacious and facile images of power as a veneer, a mask, or an optical illusion, and of revolution as a scraping or cleaning of the surface, removing the shell of the law and liberating the nature it conceals. For desire is contemporary and coeternal with power, and it submits only because it is power that gives shape to desire. We have to leave the royal road that political philosophies, whether reactionary or progressive, have always taken, and have done with the set of questions shared by gentle democrats anxious to strengthen islands of freedom and natural rights in the totalitarian ocean of the state and good revolutionaries anxious to preserve a sanctuary for desire, a vital source of libertarian explosions outside the law which condemns it. For the sanctuary exists no more than the islands do; the desire for revolution is no more real than spaces of pure freedom; and desire is nothing but power: the two are completely homogeneous.

The argument can therefore be reversed: If there is no systematic knowledge of humanity without an anthropology, there is no anthropology either without a systematic knowledge of humanity. Power mobilizes desire and manages its economy because desire has first of all constructed that economy and created its forms. Most important, this provides us with the key that allows us to escape from the dead ends of Deleuzean leftism. We can maintain as he does that power is a matter of desire, and argue against him that it is not therefore explicable in terms of a desire for power. We can agree with him that power is completely shaped by and shot through with desire, and yet argue against him that desire is nevertheless not the mainspring and the basis of power. We can agree that power touches the heart of desire, and still argue against him that it is not desire which creates power, but *power which creates desire, gives it form, and makes it possible.* And it thereby becomes clear that revolutionary psychology, in both the crudest and the most highly developed form, is always a political delusion, an organized lie, a pitiful weapon against the power of the Master. We can understand why, for example, against the great Stoic tradition —from Epictetus's advice to "abstain" to the "self-reductions" of contemporary Italians, from La Boétie's idea of desire ceasing to give suck to the state it nourishes to the contemporary "hippie" who, weary of hoping to "take" power, decides to "leave" it to the bureaucrats and paranoids—the Princes have always been able, without a moment's hesitation, to establish fantastic mechanisms of integration. We can understand why, against the great libertarian tradition—which says, like Bakunin, that there is a primitive instinct which renews the revolution's strength, or, like the heirs of May '68, that there is a parasitic libido corroding the hull of the ship of state and delaying its triumphal progress—the helmsmen have always been able to find a defense. In fact, they haven't even had to look for one, since primitive, parasitic, rebellious, and corrosive forms of desire are all simply versions of the pure will of the Master.

The same argument holds for language, and its effects, as we shall see, are analogous. There is an obvious relationship between the form of power and the shape of language, between the orders of a Prince and the images of a sentence.[2] Has an analysis ever been made of how much Cicero's Latin owes to those great maneuvers of power, Roman battles? Has anyone ever asked what theocracy would have been like if the Holy Scriptures had not been written in Greek? Has anyone ever measured how much the *Pax Romana* owed to the diffusion of a single language from the central core to the Byzantine Marches, and what the current *Pax Americana* in turn owes to the dominance of a single language, from Singapore to New York, and including *franglais?* There is a linguistic capital subject to strict rules of conservation and transformation. In this capital there is the living trace of tradition, the seal of the reason of Princes, and the deadly scar of their contracts. Perhaps speech is not, as Aristotle proposed, a neutral and pacified space in which conflict can be expressed; nor is it, as the Marxists assert, a political instrument which oppressors and oppressed in turn make use of; nor is it even, as Foucault's followers say, a critical *stake* in the struggle for power. It *is* simply power, *the very form of power, entirely shaped by power* even in its most modest rhetorical expression.

And the Princes are fully aware of this, informed by

their infallible instinct and the lessons of their tutors: Waging war is creating meaning, and grammar is a science of power. From Condillac using the word "commerce" to refer to both social exchange and linguistic communication, to the Convention proclaiming, on 8 Pluviôse of the year IV, that laws and notarial documents were to be composed in French, the importance of language as a tool and a vehicle of power was established in speech and action. From Richelieu, establishing the Académie Française and entrusting it with the compilation of a dictionary, a grammar, a poetics, and a rhetoric, to Leibniz, philosopher at the service of the Prince, imagining a "Universal Characteristic," a code of all possible codes, the ground of all thinkable grounds, we know that the regulation of language is the best preparation for the regulation of souls. From as far back as Pericles, sending the grammarian Protagoras to endow the colony of Thurii with a new code of law, to Saussure, the founder of modern linguistics, rediscovering the ancient image of the "legislator" to provide a basis for language, and the political metaphor of the "arbitrary" to define the sign, grammar has always been thought of as legislation, and legislation as working on language. De Gaulle commenting on the *Robert*, Pompidou with a degree in grammar, François Ier issuing decrees in French, Chiang Ching planning to recast the structures of the Chinese language, African heads of state attempting to substitute a unified and centralized language for dangerous indigenous languages— they are all saying the same thing in different ways: There is an idiomatic science of power, an algebra of domination, and there is no politics that is not first of all a linguistics.

Once again, the proposition can be reversed: There is no linguistics that is not through and through a politics. Language is not the free murmur, the disorderly proliferation described by so many false poets and visionary apostles of the systematic disordering of words. To speak is inevitably to pronounce and articulate the law. There is no full speech which is not full of prohibition, no free discourse not stamped with the seal of tyranny. Linguists say[3] that language is a "system" and a "structure," a network of prohibitions and barriers, a way of *not saying*, a dictionary of *unthinkable* thoughts. Grammar is a police force, syntax a court of law, writing a pair of handcuffs on the fundamental unity of speech learned by rote that lies behind the apparent variety of words. Philosophers say we must take the court of law and the police force literally; disciplined, ordered, and disciplining language presupposes a legislator, arbitrariness, and laws. Men and peoples speak because they are made into speaking creatures by an "other," and this mythic other has all the features of the Prince. And the Freudians have arrived at the conclusion that this Prince is not the concrete Prince, but the servant and the prop of all possible Princes; the legislator is the net in which all languages are caught, and therefore to speak is to become, in every sense of the term, a *subject.*

In the face of these dark and cruel arguments, what can be accomplished by the pitiful leftist slogan of the liberation of speech and the reconquest of its powers? Free speech is free only to be exchanged, and the power of discourse is always in the service of the forms of power. What was the value of the ideas of '68 about a seizure of language preceding the seizure of power, a graffiti war as a prelude to guerrilla war? The bourgeoisie was not taken in; it left the revolutionaries to chatter in the universities, and took care of serious business while we lost our way amid shrill wall posters. Who do the experts of the official left think they're kidding when now, ten years after the fact, they think it appropriate and elegant to "restore" speech to the people, as though some evil geniuses had managed to make them lose it? Speech cannot be confiscated, no one gags anyone else, peoples speak—there is no end to their talk—but they have never stopped speaking the language of their masters. Do the owls of official Marxism and the squirrels of the leftist vulgate know what they're saying, do they even know what it means to speak, when they repeat again the old refrain about the inaudible murmur of the masses and the evil of its reticence? We hear nothing but that murmur from one end of the planet to the other, and I know nothing more talkative than this supposed reticence. From the practice of "confession" to the State leftism of Giscard, rulers have never done anything but piously listen to the words of the ruled. Fascination with China has definitely outlived its usefulness, and misunderstanding of the cultural revolution especially has gone on too long. If we reduce the concept of the cultural revolution to a revolution of culture, to an event in culture, to the emergence of a *counterculture,* then it is a myth, the most absurd and intolerable myth, the most modern refuge for optimism.

The truth is that we have to learn to give up altogether the eloquent but facile images of smothering or repression of speech, the simplistic vocabulary of courts and police forces, and the idea of rebellious speech buried in the sands of history. We have to admit that controlled speech is no more a reality than muzzled desire; speech is no more subject to power than desire is. In the end, speech does only one thing, from the pontifical heights where learned men utter it, to the workshops where rebels attempt to undo it: it tirelessly repeats the pure name of the Unity that establishes it, desperately sings the chorus master's eternal praise, and domesticates the riddle of its insurmountable transcendence. Or rather we have to admit that speech has only one power, only one way of having an effect and shaping the reality of the world: by revealing the forms of lordship, surveying the shores of the impossible, and making the circuit of the great enclosures of misery. After all, why do we speak? Philosophers have repeated it often enough: because men live together and fail to communicate. Lacan has shown it in his way: because men have bodies and bodies cannot be joined together. There is speech because there is social existence, and social existence is war. There are languages and language because there is want, and want is misery.

5 The Order of Things

The argument is not yet complete, and we have to pursue optimism to its final hiding places, reveal it in its most diaphanous and infallible manifestations. No desire and no language can escape from the Master? There is no such thing as revolutionary desire or revolutionary language? This is because, more profoundly, there is no reality and no history outside the domain of power, no revolutionary reality, no revolutionary history. Concretely, this means that basing the idea of happiness on the order of things and the world is an unfortunate fantasy, deluding itself about reality. Basing that fantasy on the order of history and progress is another fantasy, deluding itself and us about time. Or even more coarsely: "realistic" or "progressive" politics is always reactionary; nothing good can come from reality and progress or from their oracular and evergreen authorities, nothing that can ever escape from the stifling grip of power. The slave and the rebel are eternal prisoners who, like the character in Poe's story, see the walls of their dungeon closing in on them—

exiles, as we shall see, in their safest homes.

Hence, to begin with, this question, which I will formulate in the most abrupt and difficult way: What exactly is reality and what is its political status? Politicians, of course, carefully avoid raising the question. They live with the assurance that reality is populated by *things,* that these things are *fossils,* and these fossils are fragments, concrete bits of *nature,* frozen and solidified for all eternity. History may rake reality with its claws and cover it with hieroglyphics, but reality remains smooth and pale, glassy and crystalline like an unsilvered mirror reflecting their will. Reality is not a problem, nor does it cause any, since it is there before them, with its silent inwardness, a passive and lethargic matter at the service of their calculations and open to their plans. *Realpolitik* is literally this: the belief in reality, piety toward the world, and the naturalization of its space. It is in this sense that Bismarck, for example, was a *Realpolitiker* since, unlike de Gaulle, for whom France was an *idea* and its grandeur an *allegory,* he believed in the *reality* of Germany and the *material existence* of its unity. In this sense Stalin, too, was a *Realpolitiker* since, unlike Trotsky, who by force of circumstances and because of his exile[4] saw socialism *in a dream* —literally saw it *as a dream,* as the dream of an imperative that was deferred as well as categorical—he never stopped *identifying* it with and reducing it to its *conditions,* proclaiming that its essence had been *accomplished* on the basis of the *objective* eradication of class struggle, the *material* accumulation of productive forces, and the real, *very* real construction of the new world.

But the strangest thing is that while politicians stick to this reality, at the same time they barely believe in it; this

Realpolitik is also a pretense and a deception; there is no Master who does not know, at the very moment that he posits its existence, that this reality does not exist. *Believing and not believing in it* is a paradox well known to scientists and described by epistemologists: The nature you hypostatize is a nature you have constructed; the reality you praise and honor is a reality that has been made real; the cult you make of it is valid only because, beforehand, you have cultivated and shaped it. Napoleon anticipated Bachelard when he confessed to the good Las Cases that he never had any master but destiny, but that politics consists of mastering your master, of dominating fate, what he properly called his "star." The *deception in the procedure* is the one practiced by the philosophers traditionally called idealist: Recognize yourself when you attain knowledge, venerate yourself when you revere, exalt yourself when you bow down, posit no difference that is not a form of identity, admit no resistance to the will which is not a product of the will. Our technocrats are Hegelians when they induce the breakdowns in society which they then claim to overcome, when they bureaucratically create disorder which they then strive to restore to order. *Reality does not exist:* This is understood, very concretely in this case, by specialists in marketing, experts in the expansion and circulation of capital. A product is not an object but a kind of superobject, there is nothing concrete in economics but concretized abstractions, and it's less a matter of exploiting resources than of producing innovations, less of reducing real scarcity than of producing fictive scarcity. Against the naïve we have to restore the truth of the market as an organized mirage, a programmed fantasmagoria, an infernal workshop where the heaven of ideas is embodied. Against those who maintain that capitalism is "possessed" and "libidinal," we have to place in opposition an "artistic" and "aesthetic" capital, which does not so much unleash energy as produce images and forms.

Consequently we once again have to do away with the banal notion that society is "denatured" and "disenchanted" by power. Nature does not exist if reality does not exist and there is no primitive enchantment of the world on the verge of decline. We must therefore give up picturing the bourgeoisie with the features of a Lucifer sterilizing the universe and burying its origins: there is no hidden origin, no morning dew dried up by a premature twilight. We must also break with the metaphysics of the property, the foundation, and the infrastructure[5]—as though there were a *property* of the world that had been forgotten and could be rediscovered. This tenacious optimism continues to imagine an immemorial spark quickly extinguished by the *logos,* distant angelic choirs that have long been silent, an archaic poem which gives evidence, in our present distress, that man is fundamentally rooted in a world untainted by sorrow. For the problem does not lie there; it is infinitely more radical: Power does not appropriate the world; it continually *engenders* it in all its dimensions. It does not *expropriate* men and their homes; it *places them under house arrest,* deepens and fortifies the niches where they literally take root. Far from malignantly tearing the thread of their social fabric, power is what weaves the cloth of every reality. The world is not what it unmakes only to remake it later, but on the contrary, what it makes, without model or precedent. This is the most difficult notion, the harshest thesis of a consistent pessimism: it is not *this reality* that the Master corrodes and denudes, but *the very form of reality,* always engendered by him. If the reality of capital, as we know, provokes despair, it is useless to place our dreams and hopes in another reality. In a word, power has the property, the function, and the vocation of shaping and designing reality as such.

We should reread Nietzsche[6] in this perspective. He was the first to anticipate this truth, and he helps us think through the essence of its pessimism. We should reread him agreeing to set aside for the moment the solid fund of "naturalism" that obviously haunts his writings. We can read "power" when he says "reactive forces," and recognize the seal of what I call the "Master" in his description of the process of "decadence." This process is sometimes a development that freezes, fixes, and arranges "active forces" as "reactive" condensations, and records the fluid movement of the first on the rigid surfaces of the second. It is sometimes, on the contrary, a decisive gesture dissolving and decomposing "positive" hierarchies into "negative" fragments, breaking them down into granular form. In other words, at times it is a movement that ossifies, constructs, and organizes a process of development hostile to any kind of ordered arrangement. At others, on the contrary, it is a movement that undoes, breaks down, and disorganizes wholes that are hostile to any form of decomposition. Concretely, this means in both cases, with the greatest integration as with the greatest disintegration, in the case of "monocephalic" organization as in the case of "polycephalic" disorganization,[7] that power never does anything but put props together or take them apart, build with elements, or break things down into their elements,

produce atoms or reduce things to atoms. Still more concretely, in opposition to the perspective, the lie, the
fiction, contrary to the artistic, playful, gambling style of
Zarathustra, the man of power, the upholder of the state,
never does anything but concretize things, carry them
out, *make them real.* Reality is not the place he domi-
nates, surveys, or deforms, but the space he marks out and
populates, the theater he erects before he traverses it. In
an almost Kantian sense, his reality is the *a priori form of
reality.*

This again explains the mistake of the progressives who,
taken in by the Master's assumed humility, taking literally
his proclaimed submission to a pseudo "order of the
world," believing the sweet fable of the alleged "constraints" under which he says he struggles, fail to see that
behind his humility there lies the prodigious ambition of
a demiurge that *he* is the order of things, and that he is
the one who sets up the constraints. He is no longer the
rival of civil society but of God himself, the prime mover
of the planet. "You will be like gods," said Hitler to the
German nation, unknowingly giving extreme expression
to the most profound truth of power. It explains the mistake of the utopians who postulate a reality outside the
nets of power, wager on a reality which power could be
forced to surrender, and fantasize a place no longer
stamped with the seal of power's will. They, too, under-
estimate its infinite strength, and forget that there is no
area that does not bear its seal, no reality where it has not
deployed the army of its institutions. Desert, run away:
that's the slogan of our new utopians, nomads and deca-
dents wandering from Vincennes to Corrèze. But they
are simply repeating old Stoic adages, without their gran-

deur, abjectly. Finally, of course, it explains the poverty of the ecological dream, and of fashionable theories like Moscovici's "growth of savagery" or Illich's "conviviality." In this stricken world, there are only black mornings, twilights without dawn, and nature is even more livid than the culture it apes. Why don't they reread Rimbaud's admirable intuition recorded in *Une Saison en enfer,* the description of this world laid waste even in its best-preserved corners, of sterile, chattering, deathly reality that leaves no way out but totally desperate flight: "My day is done; I am leaving Europe." To do what? Business, that is, technology again, and the fulfillment of reality.

6   History Does Not Exist

The same argument holds for history, which also does not escape from the nets of power and provides no better refuge for rebellion than reality does. There are countless optimists, armed with the "memory" of struggles, a "philosophy" of history, and an unshakable faith in its essential "progressivism," who make of history the surest support for their hope for a better world. This optimism is foolish, and here is why.

First of all, as with reality, history quite simply does not exist. This paradoxical assertion has been made by historians for several decades, and they have in a sense proved it.[8] They have said again and again that history was never the raw material of their work, the assumption behind their research, the *a priori* of their discourse, but always the result, the final statement of that discourse, the object produced by their work. An historical analysis is never a simple treatment, translation, or even transformation of given documents changed into monuments, but, as Roussel said, a "movement of reorganization," a "circuit of the graveyard that creates by destroying." The archives themselves, from which historians draw their data, are a veritable workshop, a technological complex in which strange artifacts are made, mixtures of the scholar's will, the library's location, the practices of collection, and the techniques of deciphering. The librarian does not preserve, he really establishes, and collecting means overturning and reordering the supposed order of things. Finally, deciphering presupposes the construction of languages, the production of techniques, and the establishment of signs. The historian never makes a silent past speak; he establishes as an event the hypothetical basis for the organization of material he is attempting to work out. He does not explain the unexplained; he integrates it into a series of abstract intelligible statements in which it takes its place as a limit, a pivot, or a link. There is no past at all, but an operation, both rigorous and aleatory, which produces the reality it talks about and the ground on which it stands.

Poets and novelists knew this long ago and drew their bitter and painful conclusions from it. From Mme. de Lafayette in *La Princesse de Clèves* and *L'Histoire de Gonsalve*, presenting the tragedy of duty defined as a "scruple from the past," and that scruple as the incapacity to give to the brutal and fatal moment of passion any real duration, depth in the past, and projection into the future; to Laclos, whose *Liaisons dangereuses* presents the recognition of the impossibility of a pure project of seduction, freed from the risks of the moment, the tricks of passion, and the unforeseeable contingency of an unprogrammed time; French literature has done nothing but tirelessly seek an impossible mastery over a history that slips through its fingers. Balzac confided to Mme. Hanska his ideas for historical novels and his admiration for Walter Scott, but he gave up his project, as we know, not so much because of the difficulty of the task, temporal distance, and the inaccessible character of a past that was gone and forever buried in the memories of libraries, but much more because this history to be written is a history that does not exist, the forgotten past is a past without distance, and time itself is never anything but space, indefinitely reversible, senseless, and indifferent.

Finally, nobody understood more clearly than Proust[9] to what extent time was a void, history discontinuous, and the past pure nonbeing—a ruin of fragments of oblivion, the simple sight of which produces vertigo. Nobody wrote better than he about undiscoverable time, definitively lost in a labyrinth of gaps, a ruin of fragments, in the *space* of its exclusions and resurrections. The road to Méséglise and the road to Guermantes are irremediably doomed to be forever enclosed in the separate worlds of two different afternoons. There, too, history does not exist, except to be memorized, called forth, and reconstructed in the form of an artifice which—like the bell tower the vicar of Combray predicts will one day permit the simultaneous vision of "things one can usually see only one after the other"—grants to the narrator and to us after him an improvised reconstitution.

From this arises the central question which silently governs the practice of historians and which the novelists' enterprise unknowingly presupposes: If history does not exist, and if, strictly speaking, only the work of men, artificially, gives it a pattern; if the past does not exist, and if there is only a senseless and random labyrinth of mud, then how did it come about that the West forged a memory for itself, worked so insistently to give itself an historical soul, and nourished the illusion that time is irreversible, totalized, and full of meaning? An unfathomable mystery about which, after all, we know very little, since it is tied up with the very existence of societies and their most archaic, primordial genealogy.

At least we can propose the following, if only in the manner of a myth. The first known history is the history of *dynasties.* The first historians in the West were no doubt historiographers of kings. It is with the desire to follow the wanderings of royal blood through the centuries, to provide documentary evidence of the origin of its ancestors, to establish its rights and its legitimacy in duration, that there was born the idea of time that unrolls, flows from a beginning to an end, by virtue of an obscure but certain necessity. Or else we can say that this practice took the form familiar to us today with the creation of the state, the ancient *polis.* In Athens, as a function of Athens and Sparta, at the moment of the Peloponnesian War, the Greek world began to move away from mythical discourse, and without yet inventing the modern concept of causality, it created the idea of linear time, rationally drawn out, and the basis of the duration of a history. We can locate the center, the focus of the history of the Roman Empire, in Rome with Caesar, and not in Macedonia, for example, the center of the Roman Empire as history, of a world subject to the law of a totalized time, organized by chronology and dependent on a *telos.* Or finally, we can say that ethnologists, speaking of peoples "without history," have never provided any notion of them but the one the ancient world was already using about its "barbarians." Lévi-Strauss, Clastres, and Balandier always speak of peoples without a state, without cities, without writing—in other words, deprived of the insignia of power, without which the establishments of men have no necessity, and without which their vicissitudes are reduced to pure contingency. These are different ways of saying that where there is history, where there is the historical will to bend the disorder of events into the order of linear time, there is always, in one way or another, the mark of the claws of lordship.

They are also different ways of saying that wherever there is a Master, wherever there is domination and consequently servitude, there is always, in one way or another, manipulation of time, careful work on time, and methodical management of its unrolling and its chronology. We should reread in this perspective the historians of the decline of the Hellenic world. The fact that Greece failed to form a coalition against the enemy, and the cities abdicated in the face of Philip, was not only the result of economic crisis or political decadence, nor was it only the result of moral degradation or military defeat. It was also, more profoundly, because Athens was never able to unify the *calendars* of its cities, it was never able to construct and institute time, the times of its empire.

Closer to us, there is Malaparte, for whom, very explicitly, the only definition of power, of the seizure and conquest of power, is the seizure and conquest of time, the proclamation by a few men of a society's historical discourse about itself. What in fact did the members of the Convention do after overthrowing the Girondists and confirming the fall of the monarchy? They invented a new calendar and established the organization of the Republic on the basis of a new organization of time. What did Napoleon do after Brumaire when he learned the lessons of Thermidor and froze the course of the Revolution? He carefully refrained from touching that accomplishment of the Convention, and he continued long after to recite the epic of his reign according to the liturgical order of the secular calendar.

And if we reread Lenin, we shall see that political action and strategy are first of all matters of *chronology.* The famous "weak link" is the weakest link in a temporal chain. Taking power means first of all mastering the inflections and the caesuras, the gaps and the opportunities that give the course of history its rhythm. On October 5, what was his response to Volodarsky, who was afraid to precipitate events? "Waiting is a crime," and we have to act immediately, *"without losing a minute."* What did he say on October 8 to the Bolshevik delegates from the soviets of the northern region? "The time is such that temporizing means certain death." And on October 15 to Yoffe, who was also skeptical about the calendar of urgent actions? The "hour" of insurrection is a political question, entirely a political question; *the very heart of politics* consists in knowing how to determine that hour. The revolutionary is a clockmaker, and history in the making is an operation performed on history as it is spoken. This explains Solzhenitsyn's famous apostrophe, a half century later, to Lenin's heirs, founders of the new age, apostles of another history: "clean your clocks," it is time to change time.

The most eloquent example is no doubt that of the bourgeoisie. Nor is it an accident that its rise coincided with the rise of a new history. It was inevitable that the bourgeoisie overturn our relationship to time to the exact degree that it revolutionized the relationship of the world to the rules of power. If *capitalism* is in fact nothing but a policy of saving, an economy of multiplicity, a religion of accumulation, then in order to take effect it needed the theater of history, which also held its moments in reserve, multiplied its events, and accumulated, if not capital, at least traces and stages. In other words, it had to break with the metaphysics of the cycle or of reversibility, which, following Plato and the Middle Ages, admitted the possibility of retreat, return, or decadence. It needed to take its place in the modern framework, invented by Vico and Hegel, of a history seen as linear and irreversible memory. And the *market*—that mysterious image of fundamental disorder which, spontaneously and miraculously, always leads to a final order; the place where the most senseless of localized microdecisions always end up making sense in the macrocosmic harmony of an entire universe—the market also presupposed the construction of a history which, though wandering and confused in the swamps of reality, lost and blinded in the darkness of random events, nevertheless constantly moves toward simplicity, unity, and order in the reflected light of a future which governs the past. No "market" is possible if you believe, like Nietzsche or the Greek Sophists, in the essential irregularity of the course of events and the behavior of men. The market is unthinkable without the hidden conviction that everything tends toward the best, that the world is constantly reducing its entropy, that history has a *meaning*—as Leibniz said.

And finally, if *imperialism* is the truth of capitalism, if it consists of a broadening of the laws of capitalism, and it operates by universalizing them and spreading them throughout the world, that universalization presupposes the universalization of time and of the history in which they unfold. The Greeks did not invent imperialism, because they believed in geography and lived with the illusion that there were scattered and particular times, appropriate for each substance and each particular place. The Athenian Confederation was not and could not be imperialist in our sense of the word, because its supporters thought that time did not exist and that Thebes, Athens, and Sparta each had its own natural chronology, almost like a substance. The moderns, on the other hand, were able to invent the idea of empire because they no longer believed in nature or geography, but in an infinite, uniform, and homogeneous space, reduced to a single law of identical temporality. Jules Ferry and the Radicals had to colonize Africa and Indochina because, as faithful disciples of the Enlightenment, they cherished a different illusion—that there was an enormous clock ticking from one end to the other of the lands not yet explored, what Marx called universal history. The bourgeoisie has power only because it has power over time; it has control over the world because it has control over history. And history in modern times is no freer than reality from the nets of capital.

There are a number of possible objections to this argument. The history I am describing was not invented by the bourgeoisie; in any case, it existed before them. The idea of a meaning in history, starting from the beginning and traveling toward an end, was already assured in the work of theologians by the revelation of the promise of redemption. Between Augustine and Hegel, Joachim of

Floris and Marx, there is more a continuity than a genuine break. The trace of the idea of an irreversible, linear history can already be found in one or another medieval text, reading genealogies as the basis for a line of succession. And finally, from the Peloponnesian War to Michelet's *Histoire de France,* the only development is a refinement and perfection of classical methods. To which I answer that the history of the bourgeoisie, the history it has promoted, is distinguished in at least two respects from the schemata that came before it. First, although Christians did conceive of something like a meaning of history, they referred it to providence, to a *deus absconditus,* an *intellectus archetypus* which provided a full account of it and freed the historian from looking for anything in events but illustrations and confirmations of the divine message. The moderns, on the contrary, innovated by secularizing providence and humanizing transcendence, thereby creating the new idea of man as the subject of history. Man makes history in the dual sense that he acts in history and he creates it, giving historians the task of seeing in events less the location of his activity than the work he has created. The difference is clear. Designating man as a pilgrim of the fate he has built, reading history as the conquest of a world that is made as it is encountered, this conception was possible only in an era when a ruling class based the principle of its domination on work. And in return it legitimated the power of that work and the dignity of a new Prince who based his eminence upon work.

Second, although the Greeks and, even more so, the Middle Ages did conceive of a kind of linear history, and although they had generally broken with the conception of cyclical and reversible time, that linearity was more mythic than rational, that irreversibility was more contingent than necessary, and the history of dynasties, for example, that gallery of fantastic masks forming a funeral procession for the dead, had more to do with glory than with truth. On the contrary, the moderns, justifying those processions, and reasoning out successions, inventing with Bacon the new idea of "causality," linked the various moments of time together, scientifically articulated them in the form of an orderly chain, and produced the unprecedented schema of a true, necessary, and inevitable linked series of events. And there again, the difference and the innovation are obvious. Designating man as the agent of an interminable genesis, thinking of time in the form of a continuous entanglement of causes in which everything develops as the necessary application of principles, this conception was possible only in an era when the bourgeoisie believed in technology and its divinely creative powers. It was, in a sense, the reflection of that belief and of its efforts to furnish infinite human space. This was a dual revolution, then, demonstrating by itself the intimate connection between what we call "historical meaning" and the mechanisms of capital. And this completes the proof that history as it is described by Hegel, Fustel de Coulanges, or Voltaire, is the same as the history of Turgot, Thiers, and Bismarck. The masters first of all own time as their private property.

So that the socialists' mistake, their fundamental blunder, is perhaps tied to their most unshakable and positive conviction: their belief in history and their adherence to the idea of progress. They have never stopped saying that contrary to the "reactionaries," we have to give up looking at the world from the point of view of its eternity, in favor of its essential mobility, its discontinuities, and its changes. Thereby, they have only stepped into the Prince's shoes, made themselves into tenants of a space-time of which he is the landlord, and enclosed what is new in an organization of time over which he has complete control. They have never stopped talking about the events, the acts of rebellion, that break the thread of history and undermine the regularity of its course. But they fail to see that those acts and events are radical only because they are ephemeral, momentary. Far from being filled with the resonances of memory, as they claim, those events are only nothingness, a nothingness of memory and time. Far from forming a chain of successive stages, of irreversible moments, they reject the chains of a history which will never be anything but a repetition of the history of the oppressed. Thomas Münzer and his rebels didn't fight in the name of "history"; they thought in confused terms of the final end of history. The revolt against the gabelle was not "progressive" either. What it rejected first of all was precisely that, the linear and cumulative time which the monarchical State had made into the most solid mainstay of its power. From Spartacus to the Chinese of the Cultural Revolution, we know of no rebellion which was not first of all a rebellion against time, amnesia, a forgetting of time, a will not to know, and a desire not to last. History does not exist, I said. I should now specify: History does not exist as the project and the location of revolution.

7   In the Beginning
Was the State

What have I done, finally, by exposing the illusion of a hidden history which is nevertheless the bearer of hope and the still vital source of a radiant future? By breaking with the idea of a reality older than the oldest of powers, lying dormant in the constraints of an internal limbo? By denying that outside of and before the law, there was a pure form of desire, a spark of morning dew in the night of our anguish? By showing that there is no discourse or counterdiscourse that will ever escape from the logic of domination? I think I have thereby defined the notion which serves as a basis for every kind of optimism: *There is a nature*, a "state of nature" as the saying goes, which existed before institutions and which we must attempt to rediscover. And I think I have by the same token begun to formulate the key proposition of a consistent pessimism: There is no state of nature, *nature does not exist*, before power there is nothing out of which we must bring society to birth with the forceps of liberation. All of which implies a certain number of immediate political consequences, which, in conclusion, I would like to set out in sequence.

First, in spite of what democrats always say, *there is no social contract,* no agreement establishing the link among men, no rights of the citizen, and no duties of the Prince either. Because finally, if no desire, or language, or reality, or history existed before power, and if they provided no defense against the weapons of power, then before being enslaved, men obviously had nothing to exchange, there was no "before" when they had the right or were in a position to exchange anything. Similarly, if there is no social instinct at the source of the construction of society, then slaves had no "goods" which they could surrender, no resources of their own which they had to give up. If the beginning is a mirage, the mirage of an archaic world, which has in reality already been constituted and has always been historicized, then the Prince never has to justify himself, and besides, nothing legitimates him. And if his excellence can be questioned, if he himself can ask that question, to question his existence is, on the contrary, meaningless. The politics of the Enlightenment asserted that on one side there was human nature, on the other Leviathan, and the task of ideologists was to set up camp in between. From that narrow and unstable vantage point they could make certain that the clauses of the social contract were respected. A pessimistic politics must assert the completely opposite proposition: On one side there is the individual and on the same side there is the state, on one side Leviathan and on the other Leviathan again, and therefore there is no in between, no intermediate space in which ideologists can place themselves to bring their celebrated critical vigilance to bear on social intercourse. Because they all think along the lines established by the Enlightenment and within the confines of natural law, "reactionaries" and "progressives" end up saying the same thing, even if they reverse the terms of the equation. The rulers and the ruled are partners in a dialogue or are enemies, face to face in either case, accomplices or antagonists in a purely political exchange, a kind of barter in which the currency is the rights of the ruled and the power of the rulers. The exchange sometimes favors the Prince, sometimes the slave who surrenders. At the present time we must argue in the opposite way, that if nature does not exist and if natural law is a delusion, then there is no political commerce which leads to social compromise, there are no free individuals who choose to come together, and the state is not created by men, nor is it the fruit of their deliberations. "Society is the cause of society," says Montesquieu in *The Persian Letters.* "The whole ontologically precedes its parts," says Aristotle in the *Politics.* And Hegel's *Phenomenology* demonstrates that if there is a contract, the contracting parties are contemporaneous with it, coming into existence at the very moment that they establish its terms. In other words, the oppressed are not creditors, nor the oppressors debtors. We will understand nothing about the realm of politics as long as we persist in thinking about it in these terms. In this sense, and only in this sense, it is possible to speak of the "formalism" and the delusion of liberal humanism.

The second consequence is a corollary of the first. If the idea of a contract is meaningless, and if there is no social contract, then the question of politics, I mean the question of the *State*, should be formulated in different terms, less as a problem than in the form of a riddle. Because finally, if the State and its power are not founded on free will and a free decision, if the State is not the concrete result of deliberative negotiation and contractual agreement, then its origin becomes inexplicable, fortuitous, and arbitrary. It is an effect without a cause, the effect of an absent cause, a "misfortune" according to La Boétie, a "catastrophe" according to Plato, an event that cannot be located, a utopian event outside time. If there is nothing before the State, and if it is not the fruit of any tree, if, no matter how far back you trace its genealogy, you end up finding nothing but the bare fact of its emergence, this is because it is primary, underived, not derivable. Like the god of the theologians, it is an unmoved mover, a free demiurge supported by the pure contingency of its mysterious arrival. In other words, the State no longer needs to be justified, nor to be declared innocent, much less guilty.

I am perfectly aware of the fact that Marxists also attack the thesis of the social agreement or contract, that they lay claim to a more refined and less idealist analysis. I know that Engels, in *The Origin of the Family, Private Property and the State,* makes extraordinary efforts to establish the roots of the advent of the state in the ordered progression of a rising and ripening history, in the "objective" framework of a specific "mode of production," in the operation of the "contradictions" in which a given society becomes "entangled." But this kind of analysis hardly advances the argument.[10] In many respects it simply repeats the mistakes of its opposite. Asserting that the state arises out of social discord, it neglects to deal with the question of that very discord, and fails to note that it could only be produced by a more fundamental violence, an ur-politics, a kind of ur-State which we should, finally, now attempt to account for. Proudhon saw things more clearly in *La Création de l'ordre,* when he explained that a society came into being first of all by the establishment of its rulers, that the organization of power preceded the division of labor, that its political order came into existence before its economic order. He saw things more clearly because he anticipated the ethnologists' discovery that there is nothing in primitive society to point to or anticipate the form of state power, that it cannot be uncovered or foreseen in the interstices of primitive society, that it is produced, called forth, created by nothing. This is a way of saying—and this is the riddle—that this State, which has no origin, no date of birth, has no history either. *It is not an historical event.*

This implies a third consequence, of even greater significance, which calls into question the central thesis of the optimists, the notion that the State will *wither away,* that we can foresee its disappearance. This thesis finally collapses, because if there is nothing before the State that resembles nature in any way, if the State is therefore not an historical phenomenon, it follows that there is no history before the State, that history has meaning only in conjunction with the State itself, and that State and history are the result of a single revolution which they inaugurated and perpetuate. It therefore amounts to precisely the same thing to say that there is nothing historic before the State or that nothing historic comes to pass without the State; that history does not exist before the

State or that when the State is created, time becomes history; that before the State, history is unthinkable, or without the State, history is impossible. Clearly, as long as history exists, so will power; once the State has come into being it is by definition irreversible; and the idea of history without a State is a contradiction in terms.

This is no doubt the deep meaning of Hegel's mysterious notion of the "end of history," a thesis that is much more subtle than it appears to be in its impoverished Marxist versions. This is also probably why, although there have in fact been societies without a State, although such conditions have existed elsewhere and in the past, and although those societies have *become* societies based on power, the opposite is never true. Societies based on power have never returned to what they were before. For that to occur, they would in fact have had to *become* such societies, following a process which remains a form of history, which is in turn always a manifestation of the State. And this is finally one of the reasons, and not the least of them, for the failure of Leninism to continue the revolution. If the State is coextensive with history, its disappearance can be contemplated only on the condition that, like the Chinese, you simultaneously envisage the abolition and the transcendence of history. Neglecting this truth, the Russians could not fail to experience the return of the repressed, in the most unexpected and most brutal ways.

The fourth consequence follows automatically: *The individual does not exist;* he is always a stand-in for the State. If in fact there is no primary state of nature, and if the State is what I have asserted it is up to now, it is no

longer enough to attack the perspective of the social contract or agreement, nor is it enough to show that the herd
of individuals does not exist before it comes together. We
have to go further and say about the individual what
Nietzsche says of consciousness—that it is necessarily a
latecomer, entirely shaped by what comes before it. "We
would be wrong to suppose," says a fragment of *The Will
to Power,* that "man's organic qualities predate his existence; on the contrary he acquires all of them at the end
when he has become a free man. He began life as part of
a whole endowed with organic qualities which used the
individual as an organ."[11] In other words, we would be
wrong to think of the individual as surviving in confrontation with the State, coming to an agreement with it or
forming a part of it, resisting the State or on the contrary
accepting its rules. We would be wrong to think of man
as a tribute offered to the Master in his majesty. Man is the
product of his own activity of power, created by the operation of his own reason. The individual *is* not, he *becomes,*
and he *becomes the State.* The words which show him cut
from the same cloth as power, entirely entwined with and
woven from power, are significant. The State has a
"head," a "chief," says Nietzsche, and like the individual
it presupposes "primacy," the "I," the *cogito,* and thus the
same metaphors and the same semantic field. One refers
to the other in the mirror harmony of basic imitation.

Concretely? Concretely, there is no individualism that
does not carry within itself the seed or the promise of a
form of totalitarianism. Individualism disperses what
totalitarianism unifies, and this is called democracy;
totalitarianism is always present, discreetly limiting the
excesses and effects of individualism, and this is called a

constitution. There is no society which proclaims the inalienable rights of the sacrosanct individual, which does not at the same time prescribe the means of controlling or suspending them, demonstrating the truth that at the root of every political philosophy known to this day there always lies the shadow of Hobbes, and at its conclusion some form of Hegelianism. More radically, wherever the individual has existed, from the day the West invented the figure of the individual, he entered on the path of misfortune and dedicated himself to the spells of power. From the appearance of the Christian idea that man is an island, an autonomous and responsible figure—no longer a cog in a machine, but an atom in a network—the West has never ceased thinking of these islands as islands of power, nor of autonomy otherwise than as an image of sovereignty, nor of a network of atoms as anything but a State in the process of formation. Unlike the Greeks, we have made individualism into a mechanism which, by separating the public from the private,[12] the person from the citizen, has logically established the separation of the rulers from the ruled, the oppressors from the oppressed. With "egoism," as Mao said, we have laid out the path that leads directly to submission.

From this follows the fifth consequence. If, when the individual comes into being, he does so only as the lackey and prop of power, we must get rid of the *worn-out and related concepts of oppression and liberation.* Oppression? You can only oppress what has inherent existence; to be oppressed is to be alienated, and to be alienated is to be dispossessed. But man possesses nothing since he is possessed by the State. He is estranged from himself by vocation, since he has no property that anyone could or would wish to steal from him. Liberation? You liberate only in order to give to the self what belongs to the self; you never liberate anything other than an inherent power, an ontological foundation. But man has no foundation at all, since the only ontology is that of the State. Nor does he have "self-existence," since he receives everything that he is from outside. There is no "generic man," but a process of *humanization* in which the arch-power is involved. There are no "impulses," no primitive instincts, but an *institution* of desire, which is the result of social organization. There is no "human nature" in general which is not a *naturalization*—that is, another artifice. In the beginning, I said, was the State. And this is why the dream of changing the world has never carried very much weight in opposition to the heavy truth of what has to be called *radical evil*.

Can we say, and this is the sixth consequence, that "revolution" is unthinkable unless we break once and for all with this collection of prejudices? That rebellion is nothing other than a pure negation of reality and of history, of desire and of language? That it therefore presupposes the rejection of the burdensome tradition of individuation? This is the final conclusion of my friends the authors of *L'Ange*. It is the extreme point of a pattern of thought which tolerates despair only in order to graft onto it the maddest, most naked of metaphysical wagers. In any case it is certainly the lesson of Lardreau's excellent research on Christian and Chinese rebellions. Yes, there was rebellion under Lin Piao, to the extent that they wanted to split the history of the world in two and break the "personal will." Yes, the first Christians were authentic rebels, to the extent that they briefly underwent the experience, consciously and relentlessly, of the radical impossibility of the self. No, revolution will be neither thinkable nor possible as long as it is opposed by the persistence of the process of history, the matter of reality, the circle of desire, the grammar of language, and the personal will of the self. I know all that to be true, I accept it, and I have said as much in my own way. I willingly subscribe to Breton's famous statement about "the desperate character of the revolution to be undertaken."

But there is something more, something that also has to be thought about, so that we may inscribe it at the head of our provisional politics. The individual is nothing but part of the State, granted. But experience unfortunately proves that the State without the individual means naked violence and concentration camps. The personal will is nothing but a reproduction of the will of the Master, also granted. But experience always proves that without the illusion of the first, the second soon sinks into the worst form of barbarism: witness Stalinist totalitarianism, fascism, and Jacobin terror. Or take, for example, a badly known figure of the Age of Enlightenment, one of the few intellectuals of that century of optimism who undertook and carried to an extreme the wager of pessimism. I am referring to Chamfort, the young man who, long before the *Maxims,* dreamed of an absolutely new beginning which would not be a return to a lost origin. He was a *moraliste* who never ceased asserting that the nothingness of this new beginning had to be developed first of all in the mind. He was a pure product of despair who also wanted to plant pikes and guillotines in the depths of his spirit. He was also a *terrorist* who, relentlessly and with icy hatred, would not rest until he had pursued, imprisoned, and executed the aristocrat Chamfort, a symbol in himself alone of the shameful old regime. And he was a *barbarian* who was capable of announcing one day that he had forever killed "passion" in himself, in somewhat the same way as a violent man "kills his horse because he cannot cure it." For this is indeed the tragedy: This will which is the lackey of power nevertheless remains, in the darkest hours, a refuge for survival against the total State. Antinaturalism, which is philosophically necessary, can also, when pushed to extremes, mean barbarism. A disturbing choice, to which the only response can be a firm distinction between the sphere of politics and the sphere of ethics.[13]

PART THREE

THE TWILIGHT
OF SOCIALISM

▬

*Perhaps this is a program for a petrified generation:
Wring the neck of optimism with its smiling rationality,
arm ourselves with pessimism, dazzle ourselves with despair. This is our harsh truth which has slowly ripened,
warmed by the black sun of our pious beliefs: The world
is a disaster with man at its summit, politics is a sham,
and the Greatest Good is inaccessible. Happiness is not
and will never again be a new idea, unless we break with
everything that has made societies possible for as long as
they have existed. Revolution is not, and will not be, on
the agenda as long as history is history and reality is
reality. Man, even in revolt, is never anything but a failed
God and an aborted species.*

*This is why we will finally have to bring ourselves to
tell the truth about themselves to the vestals of revolution,
its inveterate reshapers, apostles of "everything is fine"
and the historical "happy end." We have to identify them
where they really exist, not in the fog of some concept but*

in their most concrete material embodiment. We have to consummate the parricide and take the final step which separates us from the supreme sacrilege. For this is the task *we must immediately set ourselves to: to go to the end of the road begun thirty years ago by the critique of Stalinism, continued in 1968 by the obliteration of Leninism, and provisionally closed off in the recent past by the break with Marxism. In other words, we must criticize, in the form that tradition has bequeathed it to us, the* name *of socialism.* *

---

*I say precisely the "form" and the "name" of socialism, meaning by that *a history, a cultural object* thus baptized by the West. But the critique I am undertaking obviously does not exhaust the question of the concrete choices and commitments imposed by the disorders and vicissitudes of the world. It does not exclude—on the contrary, it *demands*—the definition of a provisional politics, a small-scale program, which some of us now think can only be precarious, uncertain, and circumstantial—in a word, a matter of feeling.

8 The Encyclopedia of Lies

We must criticize socialism first of all not only because it is one version, among many, of optimism, but because it is the most serious and the coarsest caricature of optimism, a summary of its impostures, and an encyclopedia of its lies. It is entirely contained in this simple postulate: History, as it is and as it develops, in its most radiant progress and most tragic detours, is the location of the good and the midwife of the better, the certain and blessed road to inevitable revolution. In its leftist form as in reformist platitudes, it is always summed up in this key slogan, whose reactionary character we must recognize, if words have any meaning: Accept this world, adopt the wanderings of its course, follow its processions, and nothing but good will come of it; out of the most arid deserts you will make the most pleasant and fertile meadows.

A socialist forgets nothing, regrets nothing, repudiates nothing. All the incidents and accidents of history are immediately stocked in a gigantic memory of which he proclaims himself the vigilant guardian and archivist. He doesn't know what defeat, what true, authentic downfall, means; he always thinks of it as nothing but *a delay, a stage, a ruse,* or a strategic *retreat* in a mysterious battle, whose outlines are impenetrable but whose conclusion is never in doubt. He knows and sometimes admits that the horizon is blocked and the present a swamp, but like a good meteorologist, he expects better days, keeps a sharp eye for a break in the clouds, and knows the moment will come as certainly and inevitably as sunlight after rain. His vocabulary is full of exquisite euphemisms, which would make us smile if they weren't tragic. An electoral setback is always an "advance" or a "progression" of popular forces. The crushing of the Commune occupies a place of honor in the museum of the attainments (which are, it goes without saying, "irreversible") of the international workers' movement. Stalin's crimes are treated as "deviations," that is as "lessons," and simultaneously as tragedies, "exemplary" cases as much as aberrations. And even the horror of Hitler is sometimes thought of as a "blunder" of the bourgeoisie, a fatal and almost happy "mistake" which unmasked it and revealed its true face. For a socialist, there is no evil which is not the shadow of a good. There is no step backward which is not the price or the anticipation of one, two victorious steps forward.

So that all things considered, the old banal assimilation of socialism to a church is not as foolish as one may think, nor so devoid of meaning. Like Christians, socialists believe in a God, whom they baptize the "proletariat"; in his resurrection, which they baptize the "classless society"; in his infinite martyrdom, which they name the "dialectic"; and Universal History has at least one point in common with Providence: it is the location of an immemorial fall, promptly set in order by an eschatological fantasy. Thus, Garaudy was probably right against Althusser (whom so many of us used to support so fervently); socialism is in fact unthinkable without its Hegelian core. In order to function, it requires a spirit that finds itself by losing itself, an absolute whose arrival is delayed but which never loses the way, a dialectic which knows neither entropy nor loss of being. This can be expressed concretely. Under the reign of a new class which claims it no longer believes in Hegelian or Christian fables, which is the first ruling class to evade the question of the reasons and justifications for evil, the socialists are the last believers in a Meaning, made without them and against them, the last to grant to history an order which its own agents are no longer capable of recognizing. At a time when the bourgeoisie, unlike the feudal class or the masters of the ancient world, conceives of the future in terms of the pure contingency of what happens, at a time when its representatives are more grammarians than historians, more technicians than politicians, the socialists become the inspired topographers of capitalist territories, helmsmen without a tiller on the great communal ship. Are *they* the modern scribes of a forgotten proletarian history? They are still, like Marx their master, conscientious and somehow fascinated recorders of demonic industrial power. Are *they* the gravediggers of capital? They are much more its official chroniclers, certified historiographers, introducing the order of a meaning into the chaos of the meaningless, sanctifying the kaleidoscope of its production with a rainbow. It is as though they had been given a mission to hold the compass steady and keep their eye on the course, to chart the possibilities of being and check them off as they blossom forth, and constantly to keep up to date the map and the calendar of a blind and literally irresponsible odyssey.

Masters of time by proxy and through the grace of the Prince, they are naturally sterile, passive, and impotent. For *writing* history is not always the same as *making* it. And in the bourgeois era, it even means cutting off that possibility for good. It is not at all surprising that they so rarely have the political initiative: they pay for their vocation as notaries with a strange incapacity to speak, to act, or to innovate. It is not at all surprising that they function so often as *ersatz*: The price for their prodigious memory is the atrophy of their imagination. The Nietzscheans, after all, are not entirely wrong in defining socialism as resentment, the practice of resentment, and a relationship to existence and politics based on resentment. For when the capacity to forget is blocked and when you are in a sense clogged by a morbid retention of traces, you can hardly emit anything but hiccups, sighs, or stammers. Notice how union leaders call their troops *to the counterattack, to the defense* of established benefits, to struggle against *violations* of the proletariat's conquests. Notice how members of parliament on the left *censure* the government in power, *challenge* its representatives, and *accuse* them. Look at the protest movements in which it's never a question of anything but *denouncing, demanding,* and expressing *indignation.* Remember the great trials of the ultra-left immediately after '68, where bourgeois law was called upon *against* the bourgeoisie, who had *betrayed* the truth and *flouted* justice. Socialism in the end never chooses the field or the arms in its battle. It only knows how to respond, react, and retort, the final modern upholder of the law of retribution. It explains by indicting; it accounts for events by making accusations. A fact is never intelligible to it until a trial has been carried out and a guilty party has been named.[1]

Once again, the commonplace that says socialism is incapable of formulating a social program is not mistaken, for its society is the society of capital, and unfortunately not even its reverse image. Nor is it wrong to say that it is too weak to manage the State, if not to seize power at least to maintain it, for its function and its mission are something different. At a time when the ruling class fails to proclaim its identity and its claims to legitimacy, at a time when it pretends that it no longer has either a history, or a moral justification, socialism identifies and consecrates it by the very act of putting it on trial. In an era when the bourgeoisie, again unlike the feudal class, no longer says why it is there, who put it there and how, socialism has become precisely the *why* and the *how,* the reason and the consciousness of its blind existence. Why do capitalists speak so much of *initiative,* and why have they made that their emblem and their banner? No doubt to evade more easily the classic problem of their *foundation* and to desanctify at all costs the question of their eminence. But what do the socialists do when they tear away the veils of this false innocence, when they unmask the adversary and indict the class he represents? Whether they want to or not, they help to establish him and to endow him with substance. Scraping away the rust of his alleged contingency, they discover the hard metal of his obscure necessity. Why is the *grande bourgeoisie* by definition the class you cannot see, why does it never rule in its own name and without mediation? Because it has invented a power which operates without showing itself, which sees without being seen, which is exercised only on condition that it not appear. And here again, what do the socialists do when, determined to give the show away, they reveal, behind the façade, the stubborn persistence of the old, solid dynasties? Well, they always introduce into the darkness of a power which knows nothing of its roots the searchlight of their legalistic moralism, and they thereby confer on the Master an ontology and a consciousness which he would not have without their help. The king is naked, they say, and they don't condemn him so much as sanctify him.

To tell the truth, I'm not sure that resentment is the best notion, and we should perhaps give it up or radicalize it. For after all, what is capitalist exploitation and what conditions does it create for its new slaves? In feudalism every oppressive relationship was a personal one, a pure and brutal act of the Prince, without contract and without promise, and the lord was in no way obliged to take care of the serf but did so out of good will and as a simple act of grace. Capital, on the contrary, is a mode of production and therefore of exploitation, which, no longer confronting individuals with one another, but groups and classes with more or less clearly defined boundaries, no longer *grants* survival to men, but *bargains* and negotiates for it according to subtle "contracts" whose clauses fluctuate according to the state of the market. And it has thereby invented, necessarily, organization of work, class apparatus, originators of this trade, and guarantors of the contract, bargaining with power over the fluctuating relationship between wages and the value of labor power.

Thus it is evident that in the feudal era, exploitation was clearly visible in the very structure of the process of work, whether it was called *corvée, banalité,* or *taille,* easily located and explicitly acknowledged, juridically sanctioned and institutionally recognized. In the capitalist era, on the contrary, the extortion of surplus value is no longer immediately visible: It blends into and is disguised by the form of the commodity; it is masked by an abstract and universally defined wage; it no longer has either acknowledged existence or concrete basis; it is constantly being negotiated; and it can be rescinded by law and discussed in practice, in the subtle obscurity of wage rates and labor laws. Capital is thereby logically and necessarily led to politicize the working masses, to make this politicization the blemish in its balance of power, and once again to accept if not to encourage the development of movements, parties, and unions which help to organize and defend the interests of the oppressed. This leads to two remarks in which I would like you to see something other than simple Marxian affectation. First, socialism is not only a resentful response to servitude and oppression, but a programmed resistance that has been organized and instigated from the highest fortresses and offices of power. And second, socialism is not only the bad and unhappy conscience of a world that plays at innocence and immoralism, but its court of law and arbitration, the permanent tribunal where the conflicts that divide it are negotiated and resolved.

We will have to get around to carrying out the analysis we need on the function of the strike, for example, in the foundation of the modern State, attempt a genealogy of this form (after all quite recent) of resistance to oppression, and discover whether it didn't function quite simply as a means of organizing and moralizing a market threatened by Luddism and the last peasant uprisings. I don't know if there are studies on the role of unions where they are in power, in the peoples' democracies, but it would be easy to show that they operate first of all as brokers and managers of labor power, and that by eliminating all forms of property and appropriation they have become the owners not of capital, but of the proletariat. The French bourgeoisie, in any case, seems not to have been fooled, dreaming as it has for the last thirty years of creating a social democracy, of creating socialism without socialist parties, of laying the foundation for a "new" or "advanced liberal" society. And why should we be surprised, much less indignant? There is nothing there but the return of a clever maneuver to those who invented it, the reappropriation by its authors of the means of regulation, organization, and control that socialist ideology and practice have always been.

On this point we only have to reread the classics—I mean Blum, Jaurès, and the early Sorel. They agree on at least one point: If socialism is necessary, it is in order to struggle on two fronts. On its left, against pure revolution, attacks of millenarian rebellion, which arrive, they say, like bouts of fever, and have to be fixed and solidified around real, precise, and fragmentary objectives. On its right, against the other threat—no less dangerous, of course, and one that has to be thought of in conjunction with the first—the threat of complete fragmentation and total flattening out of the social arena, which would be the very form of barbarism. Against the revolutionaries, who make too much noise, and the fascists, who make none; against the cacophony of the first and the silence of the second, socialism offers in opposition the location and the demand for a dialogue. It reasons in terms of arbitration, regulation, and harmony. It represents the geometric point at which differences are reconciled, rest amid conflict, economy in emptiness. Internationalism is not war. Class struggle is not a struggle. And it is precisely in order to forget war and struggle that the West invented socialism.

Let me be clear. I am not saying that, at least in this respect, it does not have its value and sometimes even its urgency. I do not deny that it can be, in particular circumstances, a possible defense against barbarism, and sometimes, paradoxically, against the barbarism it has itself unleashed. I am simply asking that we stop confusing orders and genera, that we use words to mean what they say, and that we maintain distinctions between various levels of analysis. Yes, the socialist left, in its liberal version, may represent a lesser evil in a world overcome with evil. But it is still not the golden key that opens the gates to paradise, nor an alternative to misery and our eternal life of suffering. As a basic minimum, a "provisional politics," it is no longer the royal road it has traditionally been thought to be. Yes, social justice forms an integral part of the highest good according to which we beautiful souls should organize our behavior. The swindle begins when it is seen as the threshold of happiness and the end of the diaspora. In practice, every question of social justice is an ethical question dependent on a moral good which is not the same thing as the politically just. Discredit *politics,* stick with the *provisional,* rehabilitate *ethics*—these are the three orders, the three levels of analysis that must be separated from one another, or else we will sink into the murderous mirages of appearance. Very concretely, this means that if the socialist master, here and now, may be the best or the least of masters, in a history haunted by the shadow of the Master in general, he *may* be so more than he *is* so, more because of circumstances than out of necessity.

His deep vocation lies elsewhere. Denying radical evil and the tragic dimension of history, blocked by the past and ruminating on its vestiges, and therefore thinking of politics only as a response out of which he makes a tribunal to judge bourgeois irrationality, the socialist is the historian of that irrationality, a *moraliste* and a policeman at the same time. He makes hanged men happy and drowned men beatific, he creates golden swamps, and he cleans out stables. The thousand flares of his optimism light up the corpses that we are, bodies floating like dead dogs through the swamps of power, great birds struck by thunderbolts from the heaven of absolute evil. He is the Apollo of this world, the form which makes its terrible and perennial chaos sublime, the industrious artist who tirelessly decorates it with sham colors. As an inverse image of capital and a fantasy of the ruled, socialism once again has the form of power. Like power, it is a lie, but a lie that gives life.

9 The Proletariat:
An Impossible Class

This pacified history populated with false images and imaginary paradises presupposes a key notion which I have only touched upon but which deserves further attention. The notion is in fact dependent on the existence of a particular historical class, endowed by the dialectic with a universal mission. It presupposes, to call it by its name, the reality of a being which the Marxists, followed by the socialist movement, have baptized the "proletariat."

Let us be clear. They are not the first and probably won't be the last to reason in terms of classes and to grant a privileged position to one particular class. Contrary to received opinion, they did not invent the "historic class," much less messianic politics. In fact, whoever says progress also says rising class, and whoever says rising class says motor of history. There is no optimism in the West which does not adhere to the notion of a history illustrated by its standard-bearers and which does not endow them with the highest dignity. Quesnay had his dialectical motor, in a quasi-Marxian sense: the "farmers" of the *Tableau général*. Ricardo had his, which turned out to be the irresistible and triumphant "manufacturers." Even the insipid Guizot could only propose his *"enrichissez-vous"* by extending a welcome to Gambetta's "new classes." And Schumpeter himself, as free from the suspicion of Hegelianism as possible, had *his* herald, the herald of his history, the famous "entrepreneur," guarantor of Innovation. In other words, socialism is perpetuating the long line of the old optimistic tradition. It falls into step with a history which has always been written by fitting the mold of eschatological naïveté. We have heard enough about the so-called Marxian break. There is only one economics, both vulgar and classical, and whether it is ideological or scientific hardly matters. *Capital* is perhaps its finest flower, but it is still its offspring. We have had enough of the old thesis according to which scientific socialism is a child of the nineteenth century. It took root and established the basis for its beliefs in the eighteenth century first of all, on the ground of a thought that said history tends toward the best, and that the best is embodied in one class. So that its "proletariat" is no doubt in many respects nothing but a late arrival on the ancient stage, which was quite easily established without it, and where it in turn must be content with taking its place. Everything about socialism seems to have been said when you have talked about Ricardo.

But this is just the paradox, the strange surprise in this affair: It takes its place on this stage in the most pitiful position. If there is a difference between socialist optimism and its predecessors, it is that they touched concrete existence while it breaks with reality. What distinguishes the "proletarian" from the "farmer" is that the latter *ex-*

ists, in flesh and blood, while the former, curiously, *does not exist.* We only have to read Marx himself to find this paradoxical thesis, scandalous for some, clearly articulated. I am thinking of the passage in *A Contribution to the Critique of Hegel's Philosophy of Right*[2] in which he notes that revolution is impossible in Germany because the country lacks an historical agent to carry it to the baptismal font; because "no class of civil society has the need and the capacity for universal emancipation." Consequently, this class has to be constructed *a priori,* and it has to be given by reason the substance it lacks in reality. "This is our answer," he says. "We *must* create a class with radical chains, a class of civil society which is not a class of civil society, a class which is the dissolution of all classes." The imperative says it clearly: We *must* remedy through theory a tragic shortcoming of being, we must overcome abstractly a very concrete deficiency, we must bend concrete reality to the requirements of German philosophy. A terrible admission, which hardly requires comment. From his very birth, the proletarian is an impossibility, the concept of which has to be produced and forged against history. It is the first historic class which, in order to function, needs to be postulated and fantasized. The socialists are the first optimists to rely upon an object which owes its existence only to the act of will that foretells it.

What happens when we try to think about it, to give content and clarity to the concept? Materialist or not, discourse gets bogged down in a political mythology which, contrary to received opinion, is not restricted to the early writings, but cuts across the too famous "break." What is the proletariat in *The Holy Family,* for example? The "abstraction" of all humanity, the "concentration" of a society's inhumanity, the "loss" of man and, at the same time, the "consciousness" of that loss—a home that has never been inhabited toward which we must return, nostalgia for a being we have to bring into existence, an undiscoverable, unthinkable, and ideal humanity. What is "pauperization" in the allegedly scientific texts? "Absolute," as in *The German Ideology,* or "relative," as in Book I of *Capital,* it is still the scientific form of the dialectic of the inhuman, which goes back to the *1844 Manuscripts* and continues imperturbably up to the *Critique of the Gotha Program.* It is the "scientific" justification for the mad belief that the being who is denuded, annihilated in extreme disgrace, and nearly abolished in absolute death is also the one who rediscovers, regenerates, and reappropriates himself, and since he is thereby entrusted with the most human of human essences, makes himself the mediator of a providential liberation. In effect, it hardly matters that this dialectic of the inhuman has long been contradicted by the facts, that in concrete history revolution never proceeds in that way, and that it never originates with the most deprived, the victims of a society. The Christian overtones of the argument[3] hardly matter either, or the kinship of the proletariat with Christ, about whom Saint Paul says "he empties himself of himself," the better to reappropriate for himself "the name which is above all names." For the essential point is this: Throughout a substantial part of Marx's work, the historic class is defined as a displaced being, estranged from itself, absent where it is present and present where it is absent, consequently an unnamable being, a pure figment of the imagination.

The procedure might have a certain grandeur. It might

even be pertinent, if Marx stopped at that point. For it is characteristic of revolution, after all, to elude thought and to defy the effort of expression. But Marx does not stop there, and there are other texts which say something entirely different, texts in which, failing to define the proletariat theoretically, he attempts to locate it in the concrete reality of society. And in this case, unfortunately, he embodies it in a familiar, much too familiar, form. He forms it in the likeness of an existing class, one that has only too much reality. He simply shapes it *following the model of the bourgeoisie.* On this point, I refer you to the excellent demonstration by Françoise Paul-Lévy in *Histoire d'un bourgeois allemand,*[4] which has been a bit too simply understood as a mere exercise in biography. I refer to the chapter in which she proves, on the basis of particular texts, that the Marxian proletariat is nothing but the inverse image of a bourgeoisie that has been purged by analysis of its historical and political flaws. The status of the proletariat under capitalist rule is identical to the status of the bourgeoisie in the feudal system. Their patterns of development are strictly parallel, in different contexts, to be sure. If the proletariat does, and ought to, take possession of history and of its meaning, it does so with the same right as the new merchants of the past against the *jurandes* and the *corporations.* The proletariat has the right to elevate its particularity to the rank of the universal because it, too, is an heir of 1789. The slogan "the organization of the working class in a political party" flourishes because, in this case as well, the power of the working class is thought of according to the pattern of the bourgeois seizure of power. Is this surprising, or even "scandalous"? It is certainly inevitable as soon as you claim to give content to a concept that has none; as soon as you attempt to particularize a class while claiming at the same time that it aims at universality. I repeat that for the first time in the history of progressivism, socialism has undertaken the task of defining the most indefinable of entities, and attempted to think about a class that has so little substance it can only be thought of in the mode of absence.

And yet, it will be said, books are one thing and reality is another. After all, there really are men in our societies who possess nothing but their labor power, workers locked into factory-prisons, wretched men living an unlivable life, crushed by everyday suffering. What are those men, who are those producers of surplus value, who are these props of the capitalist inferno, if not precisely the proletariat, the eternal victims of this machine that feeds on them? Yes, of course that's true. As much humanism as you like, and morality even more. But I am simply saying that between that misery and what socialism means when it speaks of the proletariat, there is all the distance that separates reality from illusion. Socialists are saying something entirely different when they scientifically outline social strata and class struggles. They presuppose not only a community of experience but also political and ideological effects crowning that community. If the proletariat is a *class*, if there is any meaning in baptizing it as such, they tell us, this is because it has common interests defended by its unions and unleashed by its rebellions. But it is also because, by its very presence, it helps to create a political landscape that would be different without it. And finally, it has a vision of the world, an original culture which enriches or adds weight to our ideological inheritance.[5]

Read the theoreticians of socialism: There is no proletariat not defined on those three levels. And I am simply pointing out that if we understand it in their terms, if we follow them faithfully, *the proletariat, alas, still does not exist.* We can forget for the moment that the community of interests disintegrated long ago; that in our new Middle Ages so-called class interests very often give way before individual interests. The phenomenon is not new; it goes back to the origins of the French workers' movement. We can also forget that our political games do not obviously provide evidence of the "pertinent effects" of the existence of the sainted proletariat; that "working-class" parties have become pitiful stratified mechanisms, choking on their bureaucratic fat; that there are right-wing parties that can lay claim to the label with just as much legitimacy. In any case, it has been a constant in the last several years that the working-class movement has come together only momentarily, around defensive slogans, and that defense in such circumstances freezes particular interests much more than it unifies "contradictions among the people." That is not the essential point. The essential point is that the proletariat doesn't have, no longer has, an original culture. Its memory has died, and along with it the tradition that enabled it to see itself doubly: as a spectacle and as a self-conscious entity. At the turn of the century, perhaps, it occupied a particular position in the economy of the capitalist marketplace. But now, torn from its roots and removed from its former homes, it no longer has an assigned position, a "way of life," or a politics. In the past they read *Le Droit à la paresse* by Lafargue or the early writings of Sorel. But now, dominated by Marxism, bulldozed by its thought police, the working class has repressed the anarcho-syndicalism which was the basis for its "vision of the world."

A well-known socialist retorted one day that I had understood absolutely nothing, that Marxism had never posed the problem in that way. He explained to me that what makes a class is less its internal structure than the struggle in which it is engaged. The class struggle, as they say, takes precedence over the existence of classes, and only class struggle authorizes and compels us to take topographical bearings. There is a proletariat, he told me, because there is a bourgeoisie. There is a proletariat, *and it is face to face with the bourgeoisie,* because there is a "process" which opposes them to one another, a process of the production of antagonisms. If the proletariat is real —and damn it, it is real—this is because class struggle is the motor of history, because all known history up to the present day has contained the confrontation between two camps, which no doubt sometimes come to terms, but which never compromise. He overwhelmed me with subtle references to *Réponse à John Lewis.*[6] He stunned me with delicate allusions to structuralism in politics. I answered, first, that I was perfectly willing to believe that struggle antedated the existence of classes, and besides, that I was ready to provide proof, with reference to the feudal era or even the ancient world. But, second, since he had brought me to it, I no longer believed that capitalism, too, followed the old rules. It seemed to me to be the first mode of production that no longer functioned according to that pattern. It is entirely organized on the basis of the necessity of pacifying war and domesticating struggle. In this commercial world based on free trade, conflict is a trap left outside the conference room which only helps conversation.

Matching references, for my part, I reminded him of the magnificent passage in *The Dawn*[7] where Nietzsche speaks of the "impersonal serfdom" of modern workers, a condition of servitude fabricated less out of conflict than out of objective complicity and the absence of "hierarchy." I referred further to Rimbaud's despairing words in *Une Saison en enfer* ("I detest every profession/bosses and workers, they're all peasants, all wretched./The hand with a pen is as good as the hand on the plow. What a century for hands!"), which are enough to discredit daydreams about the "potlatch" of which, so it appears, the class struggle is an exacerbated form.[8] The passage sets against these daydreams the somber reality of equivalence, a generalized bargaining which reduces our social relationships to subtle forms of contract and compromise. I explained to him that Galileo was the one, rather than Marx, who spoke the truth about capital. The distribution of its social field can best be represented by the "whirling movements" of Descartes. Isn't capital contemporary with a scientific revolution which replaced the categories and the geography of the ancient cosmos with the indefinite and completely undifferentiated flatness of a gigantic Ground absorbing all thinkable grounds? Living under capitalism is living in a universe where a mad rotation discredits the particular and reduces it to identity. Living under the rule of the commodity is living in a space in which classes lose their assigned places and become atypical, compounds of false variety and very real uniformity. In this frozen realm of identity, social intercourse holds in store and aims for a zero state, an absolute equivalence in which particular properties and differences are abolished. It tends toward an equation, a mean, an average, fascinated and as it were seized by a mathematical equivalent that it constantly postulates without ever quite reaching it. All characters are of equal value, and conflicts are sterile.

Very well, answered my socialist, but *distinguo.* You seem to have confused "class" and "class consciousness," class "in itself" and class "for itself." We have never denied that the proletariat never comes into being spontaneously. And Lenin already said that its natural inclination leads it to trade unionism, that is, class collaboration and the refusal of power. Nor have we ever denied that except for moments of grace, it gets bogged down in a mean, in the political shallows that have been characterized as the "practico-inert." We know it as well as you do. Spontaneously it is a mass of egotisms with the will to survive, a collection of petty desires and servile wills, so clearly described by the theoreticians of voluntary servitude. But we also know, because historical experience and theory both attest to it, that once a year, once every ten years, perhaps once every century, it succeeds in becoming a "group in fusion" capable of pulverizing the heavy doors of oppression and making itself, the proletariat, a contender for hegemony. When history overwhelms it, when the grace of consciousness comes to it, when it is impregnated with revolutionary science, it becomes pure insurrection, unheard-of heroism, and the will to break not only its own chains but those of the whole society. The working class is indeed *philistinism,* but it is also *revolt.* Although it is an unformed aggregate of desires for survival, it can sometimes be fused, come together miraculously and unleash a formidable force of subversion. The proletariat is only exceptionally proletarian, but it is the exception that counts and gives it dignity. It comes to its truth only at the end of a long march, but that is the end we are thinking of when we think of history in terms of class struggle.

This time it was my turn to introduce a *distinguo*. I willingly accepted, since it is basically one of the hypotheses of this book, the dualism of wills, souls, and histories. I agreed that the same men can be simultaneously, or even successively, willing slaves caught up in social commerce and heroic rebels suddenly refusing resignation to an unhappy existence. But I pointed out that this dualism was never the result of a reversal of desire, a maturing of will, or an advance in consciousness. On the contrary, it needs the coexistence, the debate, and the confrontation within each individual of two desires, two wills, two distinct and profoundly competitive varieties of consciousness. In other words, I stuck to the antinaturalist thesis which denies the continued existence of a good nature that has been excluded, now returning from the great distance of its buried origin. And I proposed in opposition the thesis of an ahistorical duplication, an angelic doubling of the soul, leaving no path open to insurrection that would lead it to power and the establishment of the proletariat. And finally, I offered a commentary on the expression of Nietzsche that gives this chapter its title. A rebellion, in the sense I understand, aims at disuniting rather than fusing and uniting. Its eternal slogan is divide the people rather than bring the people together. This was clearly shown by the Maoist rebellion in France, and later by the fine analysis of it in *L'Ange*. The proletariat in

power means, very quickly and necessarily, the sinister
farce of tanks in Budapest and Prague, renewed oppression for the benefit of a new Prince born on the dung heap
of lost popular illusions. It is enough to make one believe
that, barely constituted, the proletariat must immediately
dissolve and once again submit. Even its power is, in a
certain sense, the exacerbated form of its will to survive,
and therefore to serve. Yes, it is an impossible class in the
precise and rigorous sense that the act that inaugurates it
is also the act that abolishes it. It has no sooner arisen than
it disappears as a class. Nietzsche again: "He also wants to
exercise power by forcing the powerful to be his executioners."[9]

I hope the meaning of this "critique" is clear. I did not
intend to follow the lead of the pitiful ideologues of the
withering away of the proletariat and its historical agony.
For the moment, I am taking no position in the tedious
debate, which has been going on for twenty years between communists and noncommunists, over the question of the role of the service sector of the economy or the
proletarianization of white-collar workers. I am quite
ready to admit the importance, numerical or historical, of
what is called the workers' world, and I will even show
later how, although it does not embody the messianic
dream, it bears with it the fate of the West. But I am
simply saying that we would need something more in
order to be able to speak of the proletariat in the way
optimists do, something which isn't there, which necessarily isn't there under capitalist government. Nor have I
said that this government is the best possible government
or the best possible human world, that by exchanging the

signs of war rather than actually waging it, it was preparing for us the happy society of understanding and "all for the best." I only wanted to show that to understand the struggles and the sufferings of men today, the theoretical tools of Marxism do not work. Finally, I have not said that by challenging Marxian constructions—ready-made clothes for particularities they do not fit—I excused myself from searching for more adequate ones. Quite the contrary, I believe it is urgent to rethink the spectrum of our societies, according to new guides, new systems of power, new orders of concepts. Which is what I attempt to do later, in the analysis of "barbarism."

10 The End of the Gravediggers

What is the proletariat good for? What do those who believe in it want, why such a passion for ignorance, such a desperate determination not to see? Because, as we know very well, the heart of progressivism is at stake; because without the proletariat, history would have no meaning and no guiding principle; because socialism has found nothing better, no better allegory, to represent the light promised by its dialectic. But what happens when that light, the faint glimmer of our fantasies and of a tenacious mythology, goes out? What does it sweep away with it, what kind of shipwreck does it foretell, when we look directly at the sun and agree that we now see nothing but the shadow of an old pious belief? The socialist ideal collapses in a heap because it has lost its foundation. The bourgeoisie no longer has a negative term which could bring a better world to birth out of its womb. There is no longer any necessity which assures us that the intolerable present will soon become the past. The old ontological argument, secularized by its new adherents, is broken by a final turn of the wheel. Capitalism turns out to be the first mode of production without an historic class and thus without gravediggers.

What exactly are the progressives saying when they periodically announce the agony of capital? Very simply, that it secretes *contradictions,* that these contradictions come together to create *crises,* that it masters the crises, but that the day is finally coming when it will have to *surrender.* Even more simply: you cannot feed your own antibodies with impunity, nor can you struggle forever with the devil inside your walls. The best machine finally breaks down. This is an indication of the supreme authority of dialectical foolishness: Society has a motor which is antagonism, and there is no positive not eaten away by a negative force. The eighteenth century is still planted in the soft heads of the Marxists; time passing does not go by for nothing, and there is no historical form that is not abolished by history. Capital was born; it will die as it was born. It has a birth certificate; let's draw up its death certificate. No form of socialism exists that cannot be reduced to this powerful proverb: "He who laughs last laughs best."

How is it said, in what vocabulary and what metaphoric system? Every socialist is a little bit of a *clockmaker,* and every progressive postulates an *hour* when, contradictions having "accumulated," a chronology bends, breaks, and changes direction. The good revolutionary is the one who seizes the *opportunities* of time, deciphers the mysteries of its calendar, and stops it or speeds it up according to need. A successful insurrection is one that is *on time,* an abortive revolt is always *premature.* The proletarian leader is not a military leader, but a meteorologist who

pays careful attention to the weather, his eye riveted to
an imaginary and indefatigable barometer. Reread Lenin,
the political Lenin of *Leftism, an Infantile Disease of
Communism* or *One Step Back, Two Steps Forward.* You
will discover a rather shrewd conception of *chronology*
which bears some relation to the Platonic doctrine of
kairos as a bending of time that is to be "decoded" and
"seized."

And every socialist, no matter how materialist and sophisticated he may be, thinks like a biologist, a zoologist,
or an evolutionist. Capital is a *living body,* subject like all
living bodies to a natural law of *evolution.* Communism
is waiting in its *bowels,* it is deduced and derived from it
like one species from another in the same genus. Each one
has a period of *expansion* followed by *decline,* well expressed by the metaphor of *ripening.* Capital is
"diseased." It "digests" its contradictions. It "absorbs" or
"reintegrates" its negations. One day, one day no doubt,
it will die of "apoplexy." Is it an accident that Darwin is
such a central character in the dramas of Marx and Engels? Can we think of "Progress" without thinking of it as
we do of heredity? Condorcet thought not. And once
again, Marx learned the lesson.

And finally, every socialist behaves like a *doctor,* and
sees contradiction as a kind of *disease,* reducing it to an
abscess or a malignant tumor. Politics is a *diagnostic* art
which knows how to locate negativities. Revolution is a
bloodletting which brings the lancet to bear on a link,
strong or weak according to circumstances, of the con-
gested or cancerous body. Socialism is a healing art which
"cures" the flaws and weaknesses of capital. The crisis
especially is a *krisis* in Hippocrates' sense, the turning

point of the disease, the moment to intervene. And in this perspective we could reread Mao's famous text on "principal" and "secondary" contradictions, the "principal" and "secondary" aspects of contradiction, where the old medicalizing patterns function so well. Clockmaker, biologist, or doctor, the progressive is always one or the other. He is even all of them at once when he attempts to rationalize his faith. These are the three points on which criticism must be brought to bear.

First, when communists preach patience, when they ask the proletariat to harden itself and to be prepared for war, when they defer the revolutionary explosion to a moment which never comes but which they claim will one day be clearly legible in the code of capital, in effect they forget only one thing. A moment which never comes is a moment which goes on forever. A ripening contradiction is a crisis that gets resolved. A class that prepares for war is still a class that is integrated, and teaching it patience means teaching it collaboration. When Lenin rejected the thesis of ripening, gave up waiting and letting time go by, when he determined in his own way the moment of insurrection, which was as carefully weighed and subtly calculated as the indefinitely distant moment chosen by the temporizers of the Second International, he nevertheless failed to give an official date to the agony of the old world. For we now know that the moment of the soviet revolution presented in reality an acceleration of the industrial development of Russia. Thinking he was laying the basis for a socialist calendar, he only succeeded in speeding up the watch spring of world capitalism. Leninism was nothing but Colbertism on an Oriental scale.

I have said elsewhere that capital is a logic of time. This means only that there is no crisis in this time that is not resolved in its space; that there is no contradiction in its "chronology" not untangled in its "logic." Every crisis or contradiction renews, if necessary by a Stalinist deviation, the necessity of capitalist domination. *There is no moment* of revolution. It is the greatness of the anarchists to have rejected the symmetrical mistakes of the preachers of patience and the learned propounders of *kairos.* Capitalism *does not have an allotted time.* Reformists have been intelligent enough to discover that by letting time have its way, they could do without an upheaval. The idea of *revolutionary crisis* has no meaning. And this is no doubt why the bourgeoisie is the only dominated class that has ever conquered, why in this century we have known only bourgeois revolutions, capitalist in the broad sense, "antisovereign" in Bataille's sense.

In the second place, to think of capitalism as a species of government subject, like every species, to the implacable law of biological evolution is to fail to recognize what distinguishes it from every previous mode of production in history. It is to forget that it has invented a type of society which dares for the first time to deny its own death, reject absolute death, and proclaim a kind of immortality for its own soul. We have not thought enough about this strange paradox: It is the most formidable death machine that history has ever produced, and yet at the same time it refuses to think about or to represent this death-dealing essence. We have not sufficiently noticed that while the Middle Ages maintained a disturbing and obscure familiarity with death, in modern times death, more than sex, for example, has become the real taboo

and the primary forbidden subject of the social unconscious. This is because capitalism was contemporary with
a scientific revolution which, by inventing linear time and
infinite space, was capable of believing that it finally
represented the image of eternity. Further, having buried its own origins in an immemorial past, forgotten as
soon as it is past, it can only push back its own death to the
same extent, and deny that there is any end to its wild
course. Finally, and by the same token, it is the first mode
of production that has never been founded, constantly
thinking of itself as in the process of being founded, fanta-
sizing about itself in terms of perpetual incompletion.
"Civilizations are mortal, except for mine," says capital.
"History exists," it adds, "since I invented it, but I am
outside it in a certain sense, I the creator bent on the
destruction of his mortal creatures, the eternal adolescent
tirelessly killing the old Adam in myself."

It will be said that this is the way capital perceives itself,
but is it in fact like that? Don't we know of civilizations,
like the Roman Empire, which took centuries to recognize that their death had been consummated? Wasn't the
feudal era the first to aspire with its entire soul, and with
all its fables, to immobility? Yes, of course, but this is no
longer the question with the arrival of the industrial era.
For we must be careful: the denial of absolute death no
longer means an attempt to block the movement of time.
In fact, the opposite occurs, since we constantly speed it
up, accelerate it, and there is no pocket of immobility
whose resistance is not broken. Nor is it in fact true that
we attempt to halt the process of death. There is no end
to the ways of provoking it and programming it, in the
form of the "obsolescence" of commodities, the "rota-

tion" of capital, or the "cycle" of production. It is even less the case that we live close to death, as with a monster who has become reassuring through familiarity. Capitalism *lives* death, indeed it lives on death, all the while denying it and refusing to represent it. And this is the real mystery, this is the true revolution. Out of this death, which it organizes while refusing to think about it, it creates the paradoxical detour through which it affirms its own life. Out of the destruction it brings about while feigning ignorance, it creates the workshop for its pyramids. It aims for an eternity built on elements that are mortal. It thinks of an immortality which is paid for with permanent death. Capitalism is the first mode of production which has contrived its coherence less in spite of than by means of the entropy that undermines it.

All this will be more comprehensible if we think about the nature of that entropy and we take up the third and final of the progressives' illusions. The left understands nothing, or pretends to understand nothing, about what a crisis really is. Where it sees pathology, the ruling classes are lucid enough to see signs of health and vitality. Wherever it detects blockage, exhaustion, or catastrophe, others see a constantly renewed opportunity for transformation and reorganization. There are crises that capitalism unleashes the better to treat them; the history of our "reconstruction plans" proves how fruitful these *putsches* can be. There are crises it undergoes that it has not been able to predict; the history of all the new deals demonstrates all the profit it can still derive from them. There are structural crises, the notoriously insoluble contradictions that are supposed to bring it down: Consider how it responded to the decay of the idea of work, for example, by a change in the organic composition of capital. There is the permanent crisis, the one Marx analyzes, between private appropriation and the social character of production; but far from coming to a head, it constantly dissolves only to re-form later on—in short, it is constantly displaced. Finally, there are social crises, the ones that continually provoke opposition between social agents; but Parsons is probably right, against Marx, when he demonstrates the integrating function of these latent antagonisms whose combined operation solidifies the entire edifice. Capitalism in action and in fact is this, all these crises. A capitalism without contradictions would be a contradiction in terms. A capitalism without tension would really be a capitalism on its deathbed.

So the bourgeoisie is finally perhaps more Marxist than the Marxists. It does not believe in the law of commodities, but it lives it and puts it into operation every time it introduces death into what is living, every time it relentlessly destroys the works it creates. It does not believe in the dialectic, but it understands it better than anyone, echoing as it does the slightest movement of the dialectic with an internal contradiction which simultaneously undermines that movement. And above all, it is more optimistic than the certified optimists; it carries the notion of "all for the best" to its logical conclusion. In the midst of the greatest disorder it is capable of predicting the form of a future order. In a state of absolute drift it detects the first signs of a hidden destiny. We can no longer say that its contradictions are undermining it, because it feeds on them and plunges into them to gain new strength. We can no longer see these contradictions as signs of disease; we must rather see them as a silent shift in the landscape, a kind of earthquake. Perhaps we should stop talking about alternating equilibrium and disequilibrium, and rather speak of a harmonious regulation of social exchange, as in the archaic system of the gift relationship. A political explosion is nothing but a dramatic form of the enlarged reproduction of capital, and a social crisis nothing but a homeostasis in the fluctuations of a society.

So enough of proclaiming victory every time the earth shakes. A system that carries death within itself and places it not at the edge but in the center of its operation is literally immortal.

11 Capital: The End of History

So we must get used to the idea that we are captives of a world, of a closed circle where all roads lead to the same inevitable abyss. This world does not possess among its riches insoluble contradictions which can be exacerbated until they bring about its reversal. It does not even contain, and this is the essential point, a ground on which a progressive politics might stand in order to overturn it.

This is roughly what Nietzsche said when, recognizing that "the ascetic ideal expresses a will," he asked the supremely tragic question: "Where is the opposing will to express an opposing ideal?"[10] This is the theme of the entire third essay of *The Genealogy of Morals:* "The ascetic ideal has a goal. . . . It permits no other enterprise, no other goal." This is in effect the key problem of the historical pessimism which he inherited from Schopenhauer and which made him call the "dialecticians" "unrepentant gossips," "bad musicians," apostles of an ideal which is not "the opposite" of the ascetic ideal but "its most recent form." We can understand nothing of his critique of socialism if we forget that this is what it is based on, on this constantly reiterated thesis: Nihilism is such a powerfully organized conspiracy that it is embodied in a closed system, inside an impregnable fortress. Any assault relying on a negative to disturb its coherence, any revolutionary politics laying claim to the throne, is condemned to "appearance," in the very precise sense analysts give to the term. There is no weak link, no unstable and tottering foundation stone on which to apply a lever to bring the whole edifice down.

This is not true of every mode of production. Consider, for example, how the Greek *polis* established its legitimacy.[11] It needed, in its unconscious, the myth of a nature where what was outside and before the law could be relegated, pell-mell. It needed, according to circumstances, a golden age or a barbarism to serve as a matrix for everything it rejected. In other words, it defined itself on the basis of a fundamental and primeval exclusion. Or consider the Middle Ages. Foucault has admirably shown that it, too, had if not a nature, at least an antinature populated with unreason and bordering its social rationale. In search of a ground on which to stand, it found it on its edges, like a tree whose roots are in its bark. As a consequence, the Middle Ages could not function either without postulating an external space forming a ring of darkness around its borders.[12] Thus it is only with capitalism that there appears a type of social bond based on inclusion rather than exclusion. Capitalism is the first social formation, no doubt because it no longer believes in geography, to recognize no territory not included within its space; the first to no longer fantasize about a nature before the law, to no longer demand that there be a *physis* as an external ground for its *nomos*.

It even goes so far as to endeavor to include its rebels. And it does this in two ways completely unknown to earlier societies. On the one hand, it authorizes them, tolerates them, and assigns them a place. Idlers and vagabonds are no longer punished as they were in Colbert's time. Heretics against the order of the world are no longer excommunicated as they were under the ascendancy of the Church. Those whom history shows to be wrong are no longer ostracized as they were in Athens. In short, capital has no more barbarians; it has the fantasy of a universal language. On the other hand, conversely, although it is forced to exclude some and condemn them to marginality, this is still a device to reinforce its unity, one more means of affirming its coherence, the supreme ruse by which it extends its rule. When a criminal is punished, it is not he who is addressed, but his victim. It is less a matter of punishing the criminal than of proclaiming the victim's innocence. Every rebellion is converted into a factor for strengthening order. And every rebel is finally made to say that we cannot go outside the institution, since the institution is nature.

From this there follows a series of consequences, political and theoretical lessons, that ought to become the epigraph for any further reflection on the future of capital. First, if this is indeed our fate and if capital is our world, the home of our distress where no light shines, then we have to change our method, our way of looking, and our language in order to give an account of its structure. We have to go back behind Marxist criticism; it is urgent to regress, to retreat much further toward different theoretical horizons that we have long believed discredited. A strange and surprising Copernican revolution: Against all

patterns of thought which explain societies by their principles of division rather than unity, which believe that
splits are more important than harmony and
homogeneity, which contemplate development in terms
of conflict, we must restore the authority of archaic ways
of thinking which say the complete opposite. We must say
that unity always prevails over division, that conflict leads
to harmony, and that the understanding of the world lies
in identity. Against the dialecticians who believe it is good
and necessary to penetrate beneath the surface of peace
to discover the saraband of contradictions, we must restore a way of thought that is two millennia old, the canonic age of the birth of philosophy. We have to restore the
thought of the older Plato, who preferred, as you recall,
to speak of "species of government"[13] rather than "social
formations," meaning a state "unified" by a "species of
character" or "nature of the citizen." We must say that in
our history, "two" is always resolved into "one," that the
reproduction of capital is always established and possible,
and that the modern state is also the one of which the
muse says that it is so "constituted" that it is "difficult to
change it." I propose this regression because I believe it
to be fruitful. I wish for this return because I believe it is
paradoxically more to the point than the endless marching in place of our prophets of paradise. Reread the *Republic* then, our modern *Capital.*

Second, if capital is indeed this unified totality without
an alternative, this law not bordered or enclosed by a
variety of nature, this fortress that is not encircled or
made precarious by any external force, then we still have
to change our way of looking, but in this case in order to
locate the place of its insertion into the history of the

West. It has always been thought of until now as a dawn, the dawn of a new world endlessly beginning; everything indicates that it is a twilight, an ageless twilight endlessly coming to an end. We have continually deciphered its promises, prophesied its future, read in it the premise for a new horizon; isn't it rather a consequence, a conclusion, and a decline—a realized prophecy, a promise fulfilled, and a premise brought to its conclusion? We have been waiting for noon for two centuries, and noon has not come —the riddle of a dawn that never grows to noon. No doubt noon is impossible, a version of a black night that relegates it to an elusive vanishing point. Capital is the sun that comes from below and lights up the high plains with a necessary chiaroscuro. It is not an age of iron, bronze, or silver, but a new age of earth, with a sky streaked by rivers of red and brown. Nothing begins and everything ends there. With its back to the immemorial past, it contemplates nothing but the emptiness of an impossible tomorrow.

What exactly is coming to an end? A history which, with capital, is coalescing and arriving at its truth. Jean-Paul Dollé in *Haine de la pensée*[14] asks the central question: Why is it that in the West there were born, two millennia apart, a certain manipulation of language, named philosophy, and a certain management of things, named capitalism? And he answers as an independent interpreter of Nietzsche and Heidegger: One is an effect of the other, things are effects of language, capitalism is nothing but the highest stage of Platonism. What is the reality of capital, he asks, this disembodied reality, universal because it is exchangeable, general because it is free, but the exact replica of Platonic ideas stripped of their secondary qualities and of the luxuriance of concrete existence? What is the modern world, this level place without borders where the laws of equivalence unfold to infinity, but the mirror image of the devitalized and properly identified space with which Descartes and Galileo, in a final sacrilegious act, replaced the pre-Socratic cosmos? Marx was not wrong when he announced the imminent end of philosophy. Our government does not realize how clever it is to censor the teaching of philosophy. For today the entire world speaks the language of the philosophers. Capital as a whole is shaped by its grammar, and nothing any longer exists that is not an avatar of the old *logos*. In any case, this is the essential point: If capital is an end, it is the end of an odyssey that bears a relation to this long history. If it represents an estuary, it is the estuary of a river fed by two thousand years of combined love and hatred of thought. If capital is the end of history, it is so in the very precise sense that it is the truth and the consequence of the West.

There is a final consequence. Saying this about capital forces us to reject the commonplaces of official sociology, which, since Marx and Weber, by strenuously attempting to describe its origins, has been on the wrong track. The origin of capital is not and cannot be the birth of Protestantism and its alleged work ethic. It goes back much further; it has the canonic age of the birth of the West. Besides, it is too often forgotten that the work ethic itself is as old as a much older Catholicism. It was before the Reformation that the Lateran Council, consecrating the notion of penitence and free will, made pilgrim-man into a being-for-work. It was in the heart of the *Ecclesia* that there arose the idea of a community of men to whom the anointment of the sacraments grants the power to will and the duty to exercise that will. It is among the Benedictines, and first of all with Benedict of Nursia, that we find the revolutionary idea that work is an imperative, absolutely central to the daily life of the Christian. Simply reread the rules of the medieval convents: they present a concern for order and a profusion of rigorous rules and codified organization that would make contemporary efficiency experts green with envy.

Further, the origin of capital is not and cannot be the industrial revolution as Marx and Engels are content to describe it. For in this case, too, the revolution which made possible the advent of industry and the new technology is older. It needed fertile soil, a ground of fantasy whose roots and images go back much further. It needed, in fact, the gradual breakthrough carried out by da Vinci, Peregrini, Buridan, Albert of Saxony, Nicolas Oresme, and so many others, Copernicans before the fact, or prophets of absolute death. How could capital be born with Denis Papin, since Denis Papin himself was Greek, Jewish, and Christian? How could manufacturing be the child of mercantilism, since in order for mercantilism to come into being, the cosmos had to be organized into cathedrals, and nomadic palaces fixed in cities of light?

If capital is an end, this is because it has an origin that is not its beginning; because that origin does not unfold in the form of a history; and because that history is nothing more nor less than the opening out of the West as a world and as a history.

PART FOUR

EVERYDAY FASCISM

■

All the same, I am not claiming that capitalism is a repetitive, redundant, and monotonous process. I am not saying that it is like a new sphinx, immune to time and chance. I am even asserting the opposite, and this is the theme of the following chapters. Although it is, in a sense, perennial, this does not prevent it from moving, developing, and changing. If it is a twilight, the twilight of a night followed by no dawn, there is an end to the journey, an endless end, which will leave us forever in darkness. If it is the dawn of a relentless night, at the end of night there may be the darkness of death, despair, and perversion. In a word, if it has no happy end, perhaps it has one or more tragic ends. If the good society is a pious fraud, hell may very well be a possibility and a reality.

And this is indeed the century's great lesson. The horror is here, close to us: the daily spectacle of industrial desolation; the memory of the Nazi holocaust and the fantastic death instinct whose madness shattered the world; above all, the news we hear from the East, the land of our illusions, the home of socialism. We can never repeat often enough that fascism and Stalinism will no doubt have the same historical significance for modern times as the upheaval of 1789 had for the classical age. Yes, capitalism is the end of history, and to this end, unfortunately, we are experiencing and will continue to experience only bloody and barbarous resolutions.

12 Faces of Barbarism

What, then, is "barbarism," which is the name I have given to the end of the end of history? How do we have to understand it in order to see it as the final avatar of liberal and socialist societies? How can we construct a concept of it capable of encompassing all the modern dreams of death and devastation? Three brief remarks, to begin with.

First, if capital is something insurmountable and a kind of completion, in order to think about it we have to forget the dialectic, stop reasoning in terms of negativity, and give up the notion that there is anything external to it. It has no womb out of which its future may come, no borders beyond which it might change its language. It is not a swollen husk within which the seed of a new reality is already sprouting. Therefore, I speak of barbarism in order to designate a future which is not a stage dialectically derived from another stage; in order to describe a monster which is not a shameful offspring waiting in the limbo of capitalism's womb; in order to predict a *beyond*

which is no longer an *outside,* an *afterward* which is a
kind of *dead end.* Barbarism is not capital's alter ego, but
capital itself, capital forever, capital in its true nature.
Barbarism is not a mutation but, properly speaking, a
stasis. It is not even one condition, but capital in all its
forms. To be clear, it adds nothing to the laws of the
reproduction of capital, but is satisfied with repeating
them and sticking to them.

Second, if it is true that capital is not a living body
whose crises and contradictions are diseases and tumors,
then we have to forget as well medical terminology, and
stop reasoning in terms of pathology. Fascism is not a
black "plague," Nazism is not a form of "paranoia," and
totalitarianism in general is not a "cancer" undermining
the health of free societies. And I speak of barbarism in
this case in order to give emphasis to an avatar that is not
a form of disorder, to depict less a lack than an excess of
vitality, less a form of violence imposed on the self than
a spontaneous and innate inclination. Fascism neither
blocks, prevents, nor prohibits; on the contrary, it fosters
power and pushes its tendencies to their extremes. It neither censors, silences, nor gags; on the contrary, it unleashes, it forces us to speak. Extravagant, lavishly spend-
thrift, barbarism is not the *transfiguration* but the
exacerbation of capital, power not *renouncing* but *perse-
vering* in its work.

Third, if barbarism is nothing other than capital, capital
at a dead end, exacerbating its fluctuations and its most
insane impulses; if, therefore, in order to think about it we
have to break away from the patterns of Hegel and Marx,
I propose again that we reread the most unfashionable of
political thinkers, the Plato of the *Republic.* For he, too,

speaks of the dialectic, but in a completely different sense, scarcely homonymous and largely antagonistic to theirs. By dialectic, he means the idea that societies *develop* without losing their *identity;* that they create new forms without violating their principles; that they tend toward something *different* while remaining the same. And in this movement, in this process, he sees less a sign of crisis than a sign of corruption, less a manipulation of contradiction than a phenomenon of decadence. And it is in this sense as well that I speak of barbarism. In this light, the function of the concept becomes clear, and in this context it takes on theoretical force. By barbarism I mean nothing but what Plato meant by "tyranny." If there is a process in it, I see it as a process of *decline.* What it involves that is new is the novelty of a *style.* Barbarism, I said, is capital and nothing but capital; it is capital exaggerated, exacerbated, and unlimited. We must also say that it is a decadent and *degenerate* capital.

From this we can rigorously derive some of its most notorious and spectacular forms. First of all, of course, technological barbarism, the face of technology as a barbaric style of capital. What does Heidegger say about the modern world? That it is the pure expression of a long-repressed will, the brutal release of forces that had until now been imprisoned, the real development of a technology that has attained its essence. Under its aegis, the universe has become a homogeneous space, a neutralized field, a somber and dismal desert where the ancient law of the equivalence of grounds and the identity of things finally rules supreme. The machine is entirely directed toward the creation of this display, of these habitations of nothingness, rough places made plain with all individuality erased, populated by social zombies and washed-out emblems. In this regime, capital has become the lunar prince of a vast plain ravaged by *hubris*, haunted by the specter of death, and trapped in its insignificance. Is there really any question of a "crisis"? The very idea loses its meaning in this soft and flaccid land, subjected to a project that knows no limits. The world is not in crisis; it is a world in anguish. Is there still time to grow indignant and to oppose this devastation with pitiful humanist slogans? The havoc is such that humanists and technocrats, with the same authority, are the mindless servants of an empty and colorless space, a flat, limitless landscape. Technological barbarism is what is new in our age, but its novelty is a form of what is old. It is not, as I have shown clearly enough, that some good primeval nature has been withered. Barbarism itself was present at the beginning; it is the origin itself as a process of unfolding. Dollé again says it well:[1] In the great northern coldness that freezes our fate, capital is nothing but the concrete embodiment of nihilism.

We finally have to ask the question of what happened to bring us to this point. What is new in the situation, if it is true that capital has always fed on death and has never stopped drawing from death the means for its survival? What has happened is quite simply that the death it has always carried with it has changed its status. In the past it was bounded by its opposite and cushioned by shadows that sublimated its perverse consequences, but now it is unleashed and the frenzy of its activity is limitless. It has pulverized the subtle and discreet boundaries that were both shield and backbone and functioned so that in spite

of poverty and despair, the living never failed to overcome the dead. Among these limits was, for example, the
substantialist illusion, the fantasy of a nature which was
known, of course, not to exist in fact, but which was assumed all the same to lie behind the humanized world as
the ultimate and unfathomable foundation of the capitalist edifice. But that nature no longer exists, the edifice has
disenchanted the fantasy and discredited the illusion; the
bourgeoisie has ceased to believe in it, entirely taken up
as it is with venerating its own pure truthfulness in the
mirror of things. The most important of the limits was the
presence and the authority of the divine, the untouchable
source of a cosmic movement centered around him. But
God, too, is dead, he has left the place provided for him
by human wisdom, and with a final grimace has fallen
outside the visible realm and the closed world of our fantasies, carrying away with him the necessary point of reference to which technology was subordinate. No more
nature and no more God: It was on that basis, on the basis
of that dual dislocation, that the modern factory, the modern State, and the modern city could be born. It was on
that basis, on the basis of that dual abyss, that an extraordinary project could be proposed: die, and die again, and
cause death around you, for absolute death is the objective present of humanity.

The same pattern operates for another face of barbarism, another form of decadence, which sectarians have
baptized the "ideology of desire." Is desire barbarous?
Yes, when it brings one to say that "a child is made to be
abducted" and that "his smallness, his weakness, his pret-
tiness, are an invitation to abduction."[2] It is barbarous,
too, when one says in its name that the oppressed "suffer,"

but that they also "enjoy" their suffering and its "quantitative excesses."[3] It is barbarous yet again when fascism is made into a matter of libido, of a micro-libido universally distributed over the surface of the social body, crystallizing at one point and then another, according to the ebb and flow of immediate power relations.[4] I know that it is necessary to open up a debate about fundamentals, and I don't claim to do so with these few remarks. We need an authentic critique of the masterwork of the movement, *Anti-Oedipus,* carried out with at least as much intelligence as the book itself reveals. A genealogical investigation would not hurt either; it would lead us probably to Stirner and Sade, certainly to Nietzsche, and perhaps even to Bergson. But this is neither the most urgent nor the most essential point. For I maintain that a theory is to be judged also, if not above all, according to the most vulgar measure, on the basis of its tangible effects—that is, simply on the basis of its effects. There is no better criterion than the most immediate and trivial one, the type of concrete consequence it provokes in reality. Now, it so happens that things are clear, and no special intelligence is required to figure them out. From the ideology of desire to the apology of rottenness on the dung heap of decadence, from "libidinal economy" to the innocent welcome offered to raw and unmediated violence, from "schizo-analysis" itself to the will to death on a foundation of strong drugs and forbidden pleasures, the sequence is not only clear, it is indeed necessary. Go and see *The Night Porter, Sex-O'clock, A Clockwork Orange,* or more recently, *L'Ombre des anges.* Listen to the poor wrecks on the road to death, killing themselves with a final "fix." Read the open racism that used to be displayed in the productions of the Centre d'Études et de Recherches sur la Formation Institutionelle. You will know just about everything of the effects and the principles of the "ideology of desire."[5]

In effect, everything rests on a few simple premises that can be easily schematized. A philosophic hypothesis: There is desire before the law, exempt from all law, a free and nomadic energy scurrying like a mouse over the social surface. A political postulate: Capital is nothing but a management of that energy, a game with those fluctuations, a coding and decoding of their galloping liberality. Above all, a fixed purpose: to become, in the game in which capital excels, craftier and more clever, to run faster than capital, precipitate its flows, and exaggerate and over-code the desire it metabolizes. We can easily see that the procedure is identical, or more precisely, symmetrical, to that of the technicians, but simply reversed. The technician says: If we erase the authority of nature there will no longer be any limits to the rule of our law. The "desirer" answers: If we erase the authority of the law, there will no longer be any limits to the free activity of nature. The first adheres to the machine because he no longer believes in God; the second believes in life because he rejects the norm. The technicians deny the transcendence which governed man's will; their opponents deny the Oedipus complex, which fused desire to need. In one case, the substantive barrier which alone defeated the dream of thanatocracy collapses; in the other, the normative restraints that keep us from crossing the threshold into death are broken. The directions are reversed but the procedure is analogous. The objective is always to tear down the invisible boundaries that block the development of capitalist madness, and the result is always to release emptiness when they imagine and claim they are worshipping fullness. Libidinal economy is a vulgar economy. The slogan hasn't changed: Push, push harder; only happiness will come out. Capitalism bewitched is another version of technocratic capitalism: it, too, makes its denial of limits the road to a form of devastation, which in this case is called "perversion." The ideology of desire is a face of barbarism in the very rigorous sense in which I defined it at the outset; starting from an unreserved adoration of the order of the world as it is, it does nothing but make it go and make it turn still faster and more powerfully.

Finally, the same argument holds true for what, since the middle of the nineteenth century, has been called, rightly or wrongly, the "socialist" tradition. I have said that socialism is in many respects a sham and a deception: When it promises, it lies; when it interprets, it is wrong; it is not and cannot be the alternative it says it is. But in addition, through its very mistakes, it also produces concrete effects. Although it is incapable of bringing happiness to men, it can very well, by desperately attempting to make them believe it possible, bring them misery. It is not only a trap, but that trap can become a catastrophe. I will not repeat the usual qualifications. I will simply note that if we take its discourse literally and grasp the root of its activities, it, too, does nothing but articulate and embody, with the greatest seriousness, the dream of capital. It is, paradoxically, socialism that thinks it through and formulates it. Socialism names the unnamable and gives it an ontological foundation. In other words, while the bourgeoisie retreats and hesitates before the horror, socialism cheerfully depicts it, makes out of it the colors of its palette, and even the colors of its future.

Everyone knows, for example, that the classless society is in a certain sense the practical embodiment of the totalitarian dream of the advent of the universal; that a Marxist politics is very often nothing but the promise of that transparency of the self and that ultimate reconciliation which, by reducing the distance between reality and language, condemns the world to unity, amorphousness, and equivalence; that Marxist theory itself, because it sanctifies the Hegelian dream of the truth becoming the world and the world becoming the truth, ends up with an ideal which is, as we shall see, one of the definitions of modern tyranny. If it is true that capital is the conclusion of the West, then Stalinism is the conclusion of that conclusion. If it is true that the first is the waning of a decadence, then the second is the decadence of that waning. What is the Gulag? The Enlightenment minus tolerance. What is the five-year plan? Bourgeois economism plus police and terror. Socialism in power is the knowledge of bourgeois illusions; socialism in operation is an absent-mindedness of capital.

For here, too, what happens, what has to happen in order for socialism to come into being? I can do no better in this case than to return to the source, to Marx himself. You remember the passage in *Capital* in which he establishes a parallel between Darwin, who "directed attention to the history of natural technology," and another, complementary history, which would describe "the productive organs of man in society, the material basis of every particular organization of society." There are references scattered throughout his work to this "social nature," which slowly replaces the other nature with its machines, its artifices, and its devices. In this perspective, the abolition of private property never meant anything but the reduction of the smallest fragment of the world to an *organized work place.* The abolition of material poverty meant nothing but the generalization of the *rule of technology.* And expropriating the expropriators meant the complete appropriation of the surface of the earth and its consequent reduction to an *abstract supernature* which is the very one managed by the technocrats.

What is social equality for a socialist but the political result of a growth of *productive forces* which the most diabolical capitalists never dared dream of? What is the reversal of Hegelianism for a Marxist but the substitution of man the master of technology for spirit the master of the absolute? It is as though, to the old question of *being,* socialism answered with an apology for *work;* as if, to the question of revolution, it answered first of all with an extraordinary display of tools and machines. Marx is not only the thinker of technology;[6] he is also, even especially, the thinker of the factory, the only one who dared to investigate its darkest aspects. It is not enough to mention his fascination with the industrial revolution and the bourgeoisie of his time; we have to go further and say that he imagines the new world only as their truth and their most complete representation. In other words, socialism in power is not only a form of capital; it is a *barbarian* form which is afraid of no shortcut, no historical short-circuit, in order to lead societies to the sterility that capital promised them.

Technology, desire, and socialism: these are the three primary faces of the contemporary tragedy. They are the three dangers threatening the future of the West. Beware totalitarianism with a technocratic, a sexual, or a revolutionary face. Parodying Nietzsche, I am willing to assert that a century of barbarism is approaching and they will be at its service.

13 The Reactionary Idea
of Progress

I have chosen these three faces of barbarism among so many others, catalogued and examined them one by one, in order to reveal more clearly their basis and more accurately identify their common denominator. The point is no doubt obvious: Technology, desire, and socialism are three particular versions of what the West, since the Enlightenment, calls *progress.*

It has long been clear that the essence of technology lies in progress, and I won't belabor the point. For Aristotle it remains a superior form of ability, a consummate art of action, and a virtuous mastery of craft, because Aristotelianism lacks the notion of linear, monumental, and totalized time encompassing in its chronology all the layers of the cosmos. In the Middle Ages it was another name for a *habitus,* an *ars,* or a "practice," applied indifferently to ethics, rhetoric, or astronomy, because they, too, lacked the notion of irreversible, global, and all-encompassing time, which Cartesianism alone was capable of making into the abscissa of its space. Well before modern times there were luminous technological cities, laid out like chessboards and rationally conceived: Hippodamus of Miletus designed Piraeus, and there was Alexandria, Baghdad, Palmyra, and Samarra. But it was not until the plan for Washington in 1791, after the birth of history, Bacon, Turgot, and the others, that the modern city came into being, a city engineered in every detail, open and vulnerable to the ravages of technology. In every culture there have been forms of mastery and control over the environment, revolutions in mastery, and mutations in control. But however extraordinary the changes may have been, it would be an abuse of language to call them distinct breaks of a technological order, because the essence of technology comes into being only with the idea of a regular, persistent, and inevitable accumulation of progress.

That the ideology of desire, desiring barbarism, is also a completely legitimized form of progressivism is apparently less obvious, but you have only to read the texts to convince yourself of the fact. Take, for example, this remark by Lyotard on *Anti-Oedipus:* "If capitalism has such affinities with schizophrenia, it follows that its destruction cannot be brought about by a deterritorialization (for example, by the simple suppression of private property . . .). Capitalism by definition will survive that: it *is* that deterritorialization. Destruction can only come from a still more liquid liquidation, still more clinamen and less direct movement or straight descent, more chance and less piety. What we need is for variations of intensity to become more unpredictable, stronger, and for the highs and lows of desiring production to be able to inscribe

themselves aimlessly within 'social life. . . .' "[7] One important point in this passage is the "liquidation" which we are
told must become "still more liquid." This means in effect
that nomadic desire is a methodical application, a lunatic
acceleration of capitalist desire. Also important are the
"intensities" which must be "more unpredictable and
stronger," meaning that rebellious intensity has the same
nature as its opposite, with the one reservation that we
expect a qualitative change from its exacerbation. And
finally, there is the "clinamen," which, it is promised, will
be more radical, no doubt more rapid, and more contingent. This, once again, can have only one meaning: a
linearity, a continuity which, even freed from Hegelian
negativity, remains caught in the nets of its necessity. For
the real message of the "desirers" is that the new is contained in the old: All you have to do is scrape away the
surface and it will appear. Dissidence is the child and the
fruit of order: All you have to do is push and it will come
forth and be born. Politics remains a maieutic exercise,
and liberation another name for a conatus.

We have to say as much of socialism, from which the
"desirers," in spite of their denials, have borrowed their
basic framework. What is the revolution for a Marxist but
the fantasy of a break which is a break in name only, and
does nothing but consecrate the effect of a hidden and
tenacious continuity? What is the new world for Lenin or
Bernstein, Stalin or Kautsky, but the advent of a seed that
proletarian violence rips from the womb of the old world,
where it lay silently and craftily hidden? Marx says nothing different when he writes that communism is the "result of currently existing conditions." Nor does Lenin
when, instead of making the soviet the extraordinary
event of a new dawn, he sees it as a complement to the

discipline of the factory. The same holds true for our new revolutionaries, the well-named "radicals," who go to the "roots"—that is, to the sources of identity.

To be a socialist is to believe in necessity, and to believe in necessity is to fuse the old and the new into an unchanging center. To be a communist, according to Liu Shao-chi, is to impose on one's consciousness a long and disciplined training, which is the only way it can attain to purity and orthodoxy.[8] It is not an accident that Marxists are the last ones in this century who have dared to write treatises on education, for class consciousness is a matter of training, habit, and pedagogy. It is not an accident that the Marxist states are the most repressive of all, for, taking the irreversibility of progress literally, they interpret the slightest false move as a sign of unacceptable backsliding. Finally, it is not an accident that socialist revolutions have never been able to eradicate the old bourgeois principles of the separation of powers, order imposed by violence, and the military organization of production. This is because, still thinking of themselves as capitalism's offspring, thinking of their birth as a form of continuity which, although it may mark a break, nevertheless derives from capitalism, they cannot help but inherit the basic limitations of the old world. Socialism, too, is a progressivism. And it is *for that very reason,* I repeat, that it can sink into barbarism.

This, then, is the new idea, unacceptable in the eyes of a left which makes a virtue out of its attachment to the principles of the Enlightenment. This is the most intolerable thing for the good consciences of today who have made a banner from the legacy of the eighteenth century. If socialism is the sinister reality embodied in the Gulag, this is not because it has distorted, caricatured, or betrayed, but because it is faithful, *excessively* faithful to the very idea of progress as it has been produced by the West. If the new "desirers" are the barbarians I say they are, murderers of souls and torturers of bodies, this is not, as the communists insipidly think, the result of obscurantism or unleashed irrationality, but once again pure fidelity, fidelity to excess, to the idea of progress as it was thought out in the Enlightenment. Finally, if technology is the mechanism of devastation described by Heidegger, whose deadly effects we daily experience, this is not a retreat either, but the farthest advance toward the encyclopedists' dream of the transparency of the self and progress through work. The time may be near when the pertinent criterion for making decisions in politics will no longer be the one we've lived on up to now—the distinction between "progressivism" and "reaction." In any case, the time has come to see the first as a variety of the second, to see it not even as one of the faces of reaction, but as its essential face.

It should be clear that this conclusion has little to do with the critique of progress as it is usually understood. It has nothing to do, for example, with the thesis which asserts that progress does not exist, that it is an organized mirage, the effect of age-old credulity whose darkness can be dissipated by positive knowledge armed with sharper vision. Nor with Althusser's position, in *For Marx* and elsewhere, that the history of knowledge is not one of a linear process leading from a hypothetical origin to a certain end, but a system of displacements, dislocations, and interruptions, which are unequally developed and overdetermined. Nor with the theses of Jacques Derrida,

who detects in this continuity a final avatar of the metaphysical illusion, a dangerous Trojan horse in the materialist citadel, a kind of ideology designed to mask the real
unfolding of a monumental, stratified, and displaced history. Nor, finally, with the theses of Foucault, the Foucault of *The Archaeology of Knowledge*, for example,[9] in
which he shows that this ideology is the child of an age-old
anguish, the anguish of a consciousness and of a subject
who see the world escaping from their grasp, lost in a
labyrinth which no teleology can destroy, which can be
closed off by no preexisting pattern of thought, and on
which no constitution can impose the form of a subject.
These are three examples, among others, of a movement
of thought that has been called "structuralism." It was
united on at least one point: It denounced progress as an
illusion and proposed other ways to think about the prose
of the world.

The conclusion has nothing to do, either, with another
way of thinking that was very fashionable in France in the
1960s, which showed essentially that if progress exists,
and if it is the political mechanism imposed on the world
by capital, it does not operate as one might believe and
does not have the effects it is claimed to have. In this
instance, I am thinking of the "third world" left explain-
ing to us how imperialism sees the future of the planet
only in the form of a procession, a slow and patient climb
toward the paradise of growth up the entire length of a
ladder on which each country must mount the rungs in a
prescribed order and following an established rhythm. I
am thinking of Bettelheim, Samir Amin, and a few others,
proving without much difficulty the ideological character
of a system designed in fact to mask the profound diver-

sity of unequal, unjust, and disjointed developments, based on the development of some and the under-development of others. In effect, I am pointing to the old argument which finally summed up the whole doctrine of the anti-imperialist left: if you want to starve the third world, bring it to its knees, and obliterate its desire for independence, all you have to do is recite Rostow's fable of the "stages of growth"; for you may be sure that these stages mean happiness for some only because they imply misery for the others. . . . Of course, the analysis should be refined, and there would be a good deal to say about the historical function, sometimes an extremely positive one, of arguments of this kind. But I will mention only one point: For a long time we have lived on the idea that progress in itself is a reality, but that the discourse applied to it is a *mistaken* discourse.

Finally, my argument has nothing to do with a third critique of progress, which maintains in essence that progress does not exist and discourse about it is false, but there is nothing at all to set in opposition to it, nor anything to replace it with, and the world simply has no order and no coherence. This is the position of a *skeptic,* an observer sensitive to the persistence of beliefs, the solidity of institutions, and the resurgence of the past beneath the glitter of novelty. And it apparently has on its side the historical evidence that the world moves backward as much as it goes forward, that the past is often endowed with strange premonitions and the future burdened with new Middle Ages. It is the position of a *pessimist,* who sees human fate less as a straight line marching triumphantly toward the light than as a chaos in which the appearance of good alternates, without necessity, with the reality of evil. And to support it, it has the evidence of the horror which threatens us and knocks at the gates of harmony. But it is above all the position of an *optimist,* in that, giving up the attempt to introduce the slightest concern for order into this chaos, and consequently refusing to foresee and project the future, it also quite clearly states that history, all things considered, is the place where "everything is permitted." And it is thus supported by the attractions of a voluntarism which sees possibility everywhere while others see what is probable and sometimes inconceivable. There is a kind of heroism in this position, but I think that it, too, fails to reach the heart of the problem.

Then what is the heart of the problem? What is new in the argument I am proposing compared to these three critical stances? If it is true that barbarism is another name for capital, and that this barbarism is itself a form of progressivism, then we must say, against the structuralists, that progress is neither an appearance nor the fantasy of an unhappy consciousness, but an *authentic reality,* the very reality of the world. It provides a complete and unreserved account of the world, and no purpose is served by arguing against it on the basis of a presumed dispersion of discourses and histories. If it is also true that, at least in its technological form, progress drags men and things toward a nihilistic fate and allows nothing and no one to escape from its space, we must argue against third worldism that its discourse about itself is more rigorous than it seems, that the dysfunctions and distortions of development do not undermine a fundamental unity, a fundamental *tendency* toward unity. Then Rostow is right, except for a few blunders, notably that to progress is to advance toward decline. Finally, if all this is true, and if capital is, as I think I have shown, a kind of end of history, we must argue against the skeptics that advancing and declining are two aspects of the same process, and that although the world may have wandered, marked time, and got bogged down, it is now really entering the domain and the age of progress—a progress which is another name for horror and barbarism.

It is therefore meaningless to "criticize" the idea of progress. It is also meaningless to attack its "illusions." And it is meaningless again to set up other mechanisms and other real processes in opposition to it. We must believe in progress, believe in its infinite power, and grant it all the credit it asks for. But we must simply denounce it as a reactionary mechanism which is leading the world to catastrophe. We have to say what it says, see the world as it does, record the signs of its devastation wherever it rules. And it is precisely for that reason that we must discredit it, and only in that sense that it must be analyzed, as a uniform and linear progression toward evil. No, the world is not wandering nor lost in meanders of possibility. It is heading straight for uniformity, the shallows, and the mean. And in order to protest against that, now, for the first time, we must proclaim ourselves *antiprogressive*.

14 The Twilight of the Gods and the Twilight of Men

On the basis of this definition of barbarism, I think we can reconsider the chief question of our time, the one we all experience as a paradox and a tragedy: the question, perhaps the riddle, of the totalitarian state.

Why is it the "chief question"? Because totalitarianism, I repeat, is nothing less than the new and unparalleled fact of our age, its undying past, and the real face of its future. There it is, the revolution, the only successful revolution in a century which has known so many and seen so many fail. You need look no further for great mass movements, for the rebellious populace triumphant even though it has been put back in its place and savagely crushed under the boot. You need not look elsewhere for the new models of growth, society, and civilization that the modernist Princes promise you for Christmas. For Stalinism and fascism are not mistaken paths, as we in our amnesia long wished to believe, but the planetary alembics in which new forms of power have been tested for the last fifty years. For it is not a matter of reparable accidents, incidents quickly closed, parentheses soon ended, but of a break, an historical fracture without parallel, as our seismographers say; and they would do better to re-read Carl Schmidt, theoretician of the Nazi state, than to prophesy about May '68. Hitler and Stalin are the false puppets and the real thinkers of a political mutation the like of which the West has perhaps never seen since the dawn of its decline. Hitler a legislator? Stalin the founder of a *polis?* And yet this is the truth that we must finally attempt to judge.

For if the fact of totalitarianism is radically new, a break in the time of power, in order for it to come into being something must certainly have happened, some link in a chain that is two millennia old must have come undone. If Hitler did not die in Berlin, nor Stalin in Moscow, if they continue to haunt our nights and remain established in a postwar period that has become interminable, there must have been a displacement, or at least a slippage, on the stage of lordship the West has set up. In other words, the face of power must have been affected by a corrosion analogous to the corrosion that I showed to be controlling the fate of technology, desire, and progress. Schemati-cally, this means roughly that power, too, tends toward a kind of absolute death which resembles the decadent slope down which it is moving: *There is no power which does not strive for absolute power.* It has been restrained until now only by being firmly attached to a set of rules and norms, taboos and barriers: *A free State is a State that censors itself.* But the State in its totalitarian perversion does nothing but destroy the codes and release the an-cient brakes: *It thereby finally attains to its true essence.* This is the real mystery: Fascism is not a strengthened but an amputated State; it is established more by subtraction than by addition; as far as power is concerned, it does not have a surplus, but in reality a deficit.

A deficit of what? On this point, the left has an answer in the form of a jingle. Where there is power, it says, there is resistance, and this resistance restrains and controls power. Where there is a State, it says again, there is class struggle, and from this comes the determination of States to outlast their demons. Everything is simple for a man of the left: Create popular fronts and you will avoid the Nazi plague; if you demobilize the proletariat, you head straight to fascism. Fascism will not pass, not as long as we're here; if it finally does, that is because we didn't resist hard enough. Still the same blindness to the reality of barbarism. Who can explain to us, on the basis of this kind of reasoning, why fascism has succeeded *today,* precisely in this century; why at the moment of a resistance embodied in a solar proletariat which was certain of its mission and solidly organized; why not in the so-called Dark Ages, when slaves had only their chains and no ground on which to stand to oppose abuses of power? The German people certainly *resisted,* but no resistance in the world was able to block the rise of Adolf Hitler. The Soviet proletariat was *mobilized,* thoroughly mobilized, but that did not prevent Stalin from making that mobilization the monstrous tool of a proletarian fascism. Peoples are there, they resist as much as they can, they fight and they die—and nothing prevents the Pinochets from ruling the world.

It follows that if fascism is irresistible, and if, in order to think about it, we have to get rid of the concept of resistance, then we simultaneously have to recast and rebuild the concept of power. What kind of power are we talking

about when we oppose to it a resistance which is coextensive with its space and contemporaneous to its effects? It
is a power represented by metaphors of warfare, which is
actually nothing but a variety of war. What kind of power
is in question when we say that it is ruined by antibodies,
threatened by gravediggers, when we believe it to be
stopped or inhibited by contrary forces? It is a military
and militarized power, a pure *relation* of power embodied in opposing strategies and tactics, in political fortresses and revolutionary battering rams. This is the currently dominant image or formula, which has replaced
the outmoded idea of the contract. The notion is shared
by orthodox Marxists and those who, like Foucault, define
a class as a strategic unit, a political text as a field manual,
and a social relationship as a battle for position.[10] And this
is what we have to get beyond if we want to elucidate the
mystery of barbarism. If totalitarianism does indeed bear
a relation to power, we will first of all have to change our
ground in order to define the power to which it is related.

This new ground on which I would now like to stand is
the one pointed to by Plato when he defined politics in
the famous myth as a divine herdsman ruling human cattle. It is the one outlined by Comte[11] when he attempted
to analyze the modern State as an effect or a reflection of
the phenomenon of monotheism. It is especially the one
explored by the aging Freud in the admirable *Civilization and Its Discontents.* Since its earliest dawn, the West
has ceaselessly reflected power in the mirror of the divine.
Until now it has found no better social bond than the
traditional religious bond. Politics is, and has always been,
nothing but another face of religion. What were the
wellsprings of the dogma of the theocratic state but the

formularies of the Church Fathers and of the upholders of canon law? Where does the modern, smiling Prince continue to drink but from the reservoir of threats and promises catalogued by Augustine and many others? If power is evil, if it wishes for evil, if it thinks of evil, we have needed two thousand years of faith and piety to exorcise its effects and restrict its progress. If there is a boundary, a limit that has kept it until now from the slope of its truth, that limit is perhaps religion, religion quite simply as a bond and a social adhesive.

Totalitarianism is the new fact in our time? Yes, but we must immediately emphasize that the crisis of the sacred is primary and decisive. The barbarian State is a forecast of our future? Yes, but it must be rooted in the inaugural oracle represented by the birth of the atheist State. After all, the world has known societies without history and, so it is said, without power; ways of thought without science or philosophy; cities without artists or literature. But this is the first time the world has gone without a point of reference, an attachment to the divine. This is the first time it has broken away from the diffuse theism with which societies have always operated. The twilight of the gods, a prelude to the twilight of men. We must reinvestigate the history of religions in order to understand what is happening to us, and to begin to outline the definition of the totalitarian phenomenon.

First definition: *The totalitarian state is the death certificate of politics.* If it is in fact true that politics has never been defined otherwise than as a version of religion, then with the death of one we might very well soon experience the death of the other. I am not aware that anyone, before

Lenin at least, ever stepped outside the old Platonic paradigm. From despotic monarchy to enlightened despotism, from ancient feudalism to the republican ideal, I know of no politics that was not organized according to some greatest good and none that did not provide a heaven in which to represent its ideal. Every pattern of political organization presupposed a divine ground as the basis for its progress and a measuring stick for its movement through time. "Although the group needs a leader," says Freud, "he must himself be held in fascination by a strong faith."[12] Montesquieu said the same thing, and Machiavelli, and of course Marx. Richelieu, Disraeli, Bismarck, and de Gaulle all made similar statements, as did anyone who attempted to practice or to think of politics in the domain of history.

Once this "strong faith" has disappeared, the vacuum it leaves is quite obvious. The shepherd is insane and unconscious, the flock cut loose and "demoralized," and God has definitively retreated to his "watchtower." There is no longer a symbolic system to establish from outside the order of order and movement, no boundary, no ultrastructure to justify and sanctify social division, no sublime design on which to project belief and guarantee assent. The secularized State, deprived of its goal, has a choice between only two directions. Either the network of abandonment, the drift of a politics which, having lost its distinguishing marks, can no longer succeed in producing the will to believe: Louis XI could cross Paris on a mule because he believed in God; not Valéry Giscard d'Estaing, who, walking up the Champs Élysées, forgets that transparency has value only against a background of opacity. Or else, and this is more disturbing, the barbaric release of a state which corresponds to nothing, is accountable for nothing, no longer has a counterpart or transcendental imperative: It is impossible to understand Hitlerism, for example, if we forget that one of its targets was precisely the beyond, as a recourse for the subject and a limit for the sovereign, the image of transcendence as a limit to the omnipotence and the murderous madness of power.

Let me be more specific and at the same time propose a second definition. The totalitarian state is not quite a secular State without faith; it is more precisely *a State which secularizes religion and creates profane beliefs.* Hitlerism again: If the religion of the beyond is what it intends to destroy, it replaces it with something else, the religion of Life, Nature, and Hell. Reread *Mein Kampf:* an apology for death and the dead, blood and race, the soil and tradition. All this weighty and dense immanence is made divine, or rather satanic, as the basis for a new cult of the totalitarian state. If Hitler is not a consequence of Nietzsche, there is at least a hidden complicity between them, located only in this "sense of the land" jointly proclaimed by *The Dawn* and *Mein Kampf,* in the diffuse vitalism from which the madman of Sils-Maria was never able to free himself. If there is any logic to Heidegger's support for the Reich, it is there too, in the religion of the property, the foundation, and the basis, in the paranoid attachment to origins and the home. In fact, every time a religion is embodied and the sacred is wedded to the earth, every time it is made the ground of politics instead of its heaven and distant goal, barbarism and murderous madness are not far away. The totalitarian State is not a State without religion; totalitarianism is the religion of the State. It is not atheism but literally idolatry.

Another example? Robespierre's Terror and his dream of de-Christianization. First act: the secular decrees which were intended to abolish an institutional apparatus which, we tend to forget, had had the essential function of diverting and channeling the whole infernal saraband, the satanic ravings of the tormented and tortured soul, into the paths of worship, liturgy, and confession. Sade was the only one of his time to understand this, and he drew from it the abject lessons we are familiar with. Second act: existing religion was replaced by the cult of a supreme being, too much a being to be believed and too supreme to function; a religion of *planted* trees and not of the divine made *sublime,* an openly and thoroughly earthly religion which, far from erecting a barrier to the collective death instinct, on the contrary galvanized it and rooted it in the soil of France. It was Novalis, I think, who said of Robespierre that he made religion "the center and the strength of the republic," its "center" and its "strength" rather than its founding "symbol." Third act: the explicit replacement of the idea of the "greatest good" with that of the "public good." The former tolerated evil, justified and preserved it; the latter symbolically denied it, abolished it in thought, and thereby could not tolerate the slightest deviation from order, which was seen as a scandal to be chastised and an offense to be repressed. This was Robespierre again, who, according to Hegel's quip, made the mistake of taking virtue "seriously," and thus did not hesitate to punish the recalcitrant and the satirical with the guillotine. Virtue taken seriously is a dangerous temptation; it offers a terrifying image of the liberty trees. The deputies of the Convention were sorcerers' apprentices who learned at their own expense that the sacred cannot be manipulated without taking the ultimate risk.

For, and this is the third definition, *totalitarianism is a form of politics in which, for the first time, the Prince takes himself for the sovereign.* Here again, we should consider the status of Princes in the Christian West. There was no state that did not vigorously attempt to humble them, devalue them, and undermine the principle of their authority. Every society believed it was created by an Other,[13] its authentic Sovereign, and the King was never anything but his pale and provisional substitute. Every political philosophy applied itself to externalizing its basis, expelling its legitimacy, and projecting it into an Elsewhere that hovered like a great shadow over the uncertain course of the world. For a long time this was God himself, author of the tables of the law, the absent prime mover of a cosmic machine, the benevolent and distant father of the occupants of the throne. He was succeeded by the People as defined by democrats, but we must remember that it was never described as anything but a replacement for God, invisible like him (Hegel's "people in itself"), disembodied like him ("purged of passions," says Kant), and like him an impossible presence (Rousseau's "assembled people"). In the face of this, totalitarianism says, and it is the first to do so, there is no supreme authority from which the Prince derives his justification; there is no absent Sovereign to whom he must submit; he and he alone is the Sovereign, ruling without limit and in solitude over the earthly kingdom.

We tend to forget that this disjunction between the "Prince" and the "Sovereign" lay at the basis of so-called absolute monarchies. Were the kings of France as "unfet-

tered" by law as the expression would suggest? They
ruled alone, to be sure, but their rule was limited by the
"fundamental laws" recorded by Coquille and Loyseau,[14]
by the "natural benevolence" which Pasquier[15] claims is
their duty, and by the power of the *Parlements* with their
"statutory decrees" and "judgments of equity."[16] The
monarchy was indeed by divine right, but this was less a
proof that it was abusive than a sign of its relativity, the
extreme relativity of its power in relation to the divine
authority which granted it the right to rule. Louis XIV
never said "L'État c'est moi," since he was so aware that
the state was God, and he himself only "held God's place"
as a pure reflection of "his wisdom as well as his authority." He could not imagine himself as author and guarantor of the laws, declaring for example that "perfect felicity
in a kingdom comes about when a prince is obeyed by his
subjects and the prince obeys the law." This is an admirable image of mediation, which, I repeat, needed only to
be revived and reinterpreted by the supporters of the
democratic State. If you transpose this harangue of
Achille de Harlay addressed to Henri III, you will obtain
the precise formula for patriotic legitimacy: "We have,
Sire, two sorts of laws, the laws and rulings of kings, and
those of the kingdom, which are immutable and inviola-
ble, *through which* you have mounted the royal throne.
Thus you must observe the laws of the State of the Kingdom, which cannot be violated without placing in doubt
your own power and sovereignty."[17]

Contrast this with Mussolini's "Speech to the Augusteo"
of 22 June 1925. The theory is precisely inverted: the
"executive power" is the appropriate "author of laws,"
and there is no vestige of a fundamental Law to restrain

abuse of the law, and no superior authority to which it must submit. I know very well there is a *higher tradition* to which this law refers and that, for Stalinists at least, it takes the form of Marxist theory. But totalitarianism begins precisely when you *concretize* that tradition, when you *name* the author of the law, and when you *embody* a legitimacy which until then had remained unnamable. Why is the cult of personality a fascist phenomenon? Because it carries out the extraordinary act of confusing the body of the Prince with the body of the State, and worship devoted to one is also devoted to the other. What is to be understood by the assertion that Stalin was an autocrat? That instead of believing himself anointed by some sacred authority, he governed by himself, ruled on his own authority, and therefore gave himself the right not only to issue decrees but to rescind them as well. What did Mussolini mean when he declared that the *duce* was above the laws? Literally, that he dominated them, that he ruled on the mountaintops, and as high as he might look, he would encounter no ancient Text which would be the Law of laws. Again, what is meant when the Stalinists or the Chinese speak of the "father of peoples" or the great helmsman? That the totalitarian leader occupies a mythical place outside society, from which it is nevertheless supposed to see and know itself,[18] with a vision and knowledge belonging traditionally only to God. The real message of Hitlerism: "You will be like gods."

From which there follows this fourth and final definition: *A totalitarian State is a State which fantasizes itself as the founder of society,* which brings power back to its source only at the cost of bringing power to bear on social existence. The Prince takes himself for the Sovereign, and in turn he takes himself for civil society. He abolishes the distance between authority and its deputies only to be better able to fill the gap between political unity and social multiplicity. The atheist State is first of all a State that takes complete charge of the lives and passions of men. The idolatrized leader is first of all the one who leaves no haven for the establishment of division and contradiction. The *sans-culottes* criticized "wealth" only as an obstacle to the "general will"; they denounced "material possessions" only as a refuge for the private man against the citizen. Stalin believed in the classless society, and he was not entirely wrong when, in 1936, he declared it had been realized. He was not entirely wrong, because it was the socialist expression of the totalitarian dream of the advent of unity, the homogeneous, and the universal. And this is perhaps the greatest division between totalitarianism and liberalism: Liberalism tolerates and feeds on division, deviance, and dissidence, because its Prince, distinct from the social organism, both signifies and remedies the plurality of worlds; on the contrary, totalitarianism does not tolerate the slightest difference, but crushes or absorbs it, because its Prince has become an ogre devouring his creatures, the great bogeyman who expands his own body to the dimensions of society.

From this we can derive a few simple rules. A liberal State, for example, can be recognized by its acceptance of the division of powers in Montesquieu's sense, as a condition and guarantee of the division between power and social life. A totalitarian State, on the other hand, can be recognized by its blindness to the symbolic function of power, the fact that it sees internal division only as a snare and a delusion. The totalitarian order functions and is thought of as pure regulation, the simple management of the division of labor. The liberal order, on the other hand, acknowledges another role, the symbolic foundation of the social bond. For a liberal, social division itself is always a primary ontological fact; the distinguishing characteristic of Stalino-fascism is its reduction of social division to the simple technical division of labor. For one, power is the very image of the sacred, playing on its withdrawal in order to preserve the free play of the world; for the other, power is thought of only as a coercive mechanism and in terms of a test of strength between rulers and ruled.

The totalitarian State is the first one that no longer divides in order to rule.

15 Faces of Totalitarianism

So much for its design and genealogy. It remains to apply the model and make an inventory of its faces, which are not, as we shall see, what we are usually told they are.

It is false, for example, that totalitarianism is, as is still said, a version of obscurantism; false that it chooses its home in a romanticism of darkness, shadow, and mystery; false that it is chiefly a wager on the irrational and a rejection of rationality. For if its project is indeed, as I think I have shown, the appropriation by the State of the social organism, that appropriation itself presupposes the harshest and strongest light: It can tolerate no corner, no zone of shadows, which would provide a haven for some possible dissidence. If it is in fact intent on abolishing the gap that has always been maintained between the civil and the political, it will not rest until it has cleared up every dark corner and blind spot on the social surface. It conceives this surface as entirely smooth and translucent, like a faithful mirror reflecting its own image. It is no accident that the Soviet camps were thought out and organized according to a rational, quasi-industrial model borrowed from an Enlightenment ideologue, Theodore Frankel. It is not a matter of indifference that Hobbes's *Leviathan*, which, according to Deutscher, Stalin read and pondered, concludes with a hymn to clarity and universal light. Nor is there anything surprising in the fact that so many so-called socialist societies are *street* societies, where everything happens in the street, and private meetings are controlled with extreme severity and rigor. For the fascist State is first of all a State that looks: Jean Moulin is the man of shadows, and his torturers were the ones who held the light. For totalitarian societies are transparent societies governed by insomniac Princes dreaming of glass houses. What did Lenin do when he came to power? He *electrified* Russia. Hitler won the war, I said. But we have eagerly forgotten his black masses and torchlight processions, and have simply reduced them to a particular pathological example of the totalitarian phenomenon.

We also have to do away with the tenacious myth that totalitarianism is a synonym for a police state; that wherever the police rule, fascism is behind them; that where we don't see them, fascism is far away. Here again, we have to say the opposite: The totalitarian state means not police but scientists in power, not unleashed violence but truth in chains, not brutal repression but science and rigor. Whoever says total power means in fact total knowledge, and permanent control means universal examination. There is no authentic transparency without transparency to reason. That, too, was understood by the men of the Enlightenment, but they carefully refrained from working out its consequences. The later Bentham was already dreaming of a "panopticon," but liberalism had its eyes open and proposed instead the state as "gendarme," but to a *minimum* degree. So Stalinism did not invent the GPU; it invented planning, or rather it rescued it from the archives of bourgeois memory. It gave body to the hypothesis that the unity of power presupposes the unity of knowledge. And Nazism is not chiefly the Gestapo but perhaps the corporation; not the medieval corporation, which implied blindness, presupposed opacity, and turned the economic monad in on itself, but the modern corporation, which translates the disorder of the market into a controlled and dominated order, once again something that is *known*. Beware the republic of scientists! It is worth as much as the rule of soldiers.

And this is why we will understand nothing about the totalitarian phenomenon as long as we continue to repeat the foolish and hollow formula learned from bad textbooks: fascism is the end, the "death," of ideology. What does a State do when it hatches the mad project to become identical with the society it administers? It imposes a language on it, its own language, its own discourse, claiming to have found it in society and simply to have transcribed it; for Stalinists this is known as "democratic centralism." What is to be understood by a *total state* and its negation of division and social polyphony? This must mean not the State but the *total discourse,* the one it offers about itself and indirectly about the society it denies—as in Carl Schmidt's homage to the inspired speech of Hitler the "ventriloquist." What is the politics of a Marxist state, how does it define the domain of the political, this State that claims to have broken with bourgeois models? It is a politics of the word, the incarnate and actualized word,

reality becoming the word and the word becoming reality
—the realization of the bourgeois dream of the advent of
the universal. The totalitarian State is not, cannot be, the
management or the administration of things, because the
knowledge it mobilizes produces and transforms, as well
as watching and recording. It is not a State lacking in
ideology, but on the contrary, the triumph of ideology,
the location of its greatest and most spectacular power.
For ideology from that point on functions not only to
obscure and travesty reality, but also to shape it, deform
it, and establish it.

The same thing holds for its subjects, who are not the
repressed and silent men they are believed to be; and
therefore for the speech which the state does not gag,
censor, or smother. For if it in fact aims for absolute
power, it aims for mastery over souls as well as bodies. If
it aims for mastery over souls, it must search hearts as well
as torturing flesh. And how better to search the hearts
whose loyalty it seeks than by forcing them to chatter,
listening to their free speech, even though it then confis-
cates it? Kautsky is the real founder of the Leninist State,
because he was the first to set out this pattern of listening
and confiscation. The Maoist theory that truth comes from
the masses and returns to them is probably the keystone
of the Chinese dictatorship. There can in fact be no successful dictatorship without the establishment of procedures through which people are invited or forced to
speak. Totalitarianism is confession without God, the In-
quisition plus negation of the individual. Where Christianity came up against the will of the faithful themselves,
totalitarianism makes that very will the tool of its subjuga-
tion. Stalin had Kirov secretly assassinated in Leningrad,

but Kamenev, Zinoviev, and Bukharin died because of their own *confessions,* after interminable trials whose only aim was precisely to *make them talk.* Closer to ourselves, we can understand that there is a threat of totalitarianism whenever a society makes it our duty *to tell all:* for example, the danger of sexology and the practices connected to it. There is a hidden impulse toward power, probably absolute power, whenever someone brandishes the slogan of total "liberation" and speech set free: the danger of inane, redundant, and repetitive leftism. Finally, freedom is in danger when a magistrate believes it just and proper to call for an end to secrecy in pretrial proceedings: Judge Pascal, a totalitarian image of so-called popular justice. When will there be a constitution that makes the right to secrecy an inalienable "right of man," less a Bastille than a refuge for our sovereignty.

Must we then say that the totalitarian State is an omnipresent, burdensome, and colossal State? Must we stick to those other images of the State as a "cold monster," a "moloch," *Leviathan?* We must once again make distinctions and refine the analysis. It is omnipresent in a certain sense, since it aims for total power by means of total knowledge. But it reaches and exercises this total power and this universal knowledge only by making itself invisible and as it were *absent.* What indeed is the political when the state projects itself completely into the web of the social fabric? It is certain in any case that it is no longer the old Platonic model of the order of the *polis;* that it is no longer the Hegelian schema of the government of the universal localized in one point of the edifice; nor is it Clausewitz's or even Nietzsche's model of peace and war between distinct and relatively autarkic units. A state is totalitarian when, by dilating the political, it claims to have annulled and abolished it; when, by multiplying the centers of domination, it dissolves the image of the Master; when it proclaims simultaneously that "everything is political," and that "the age of politics is at an end." Its ideal image is an evanescent, discreet, and imperceptible State. Its realized image is a State that cannot be seen because it is present everywhere: totalitarianism, too, in its own way, calls for "the smallest amount of State possible." A paradox? See Lenin in *The State and Revolution:* We have to distinguish, he says, between the "abolition" and the "withering away" of the state; the proletarian State is withering away without being abolished. Or consider Stalin, who maintained to the end this dual theory: The socialist State is a state in *the process of extinction,* but that extinction will *come from strengthening it.* Once again, there is nothing more to say. The State can *strengthen itself,* and consequently absorb the body of society, only by agreeing to *wither away*—that is, to perish as a visible structure.

PART FIVE

THE NEW PRINCE

■

Capitalism and barbarism, socialism and barbarism. What liberal forces in the West can stand against the steamroller of progressive technocracy? And where is the samizdat *in the East capable of neutralizing the iron speech of the modern red czars? Like victims of torture in horror stories, it seems that we can no longer choose anything but the form of totalitarianism best adapted to the fate being prepared for us. Will it be Carl Schmidt's or Joseph Stalin's? The totalitarianism of the sexologists or that of scientists in power? The night of the concentration camp or the harsh light of a new panopticon? A centralized and powerful state or universal self-management? The brief inventory I have made proves at least that our Princes have a wide range of colors on their palette, and that tomorrow's barbarism has for allies all the resources of the future and of progress.*

As far as I'm concerned, the game is over. For us in the West, the barbarism to come will have the most tragic of all faces: the human face of a "socialism" that will take on itself all the flaws and excesses of industrial society; the reign of a wise and well-to-do populace which, in France at least, can already be seen in the mirror images of Chirac's extreme right and smiling communism; the victory of a "style" called fascist or proletarian, no matter, for which the democratic or libertarian "style" has already paid the price. We can see on the horizon a confused joint rule, a strange political Siren with capital for a body and a Marxist head; a new kind of Pax Romana; a dual hegemony whose first symptoms can already be detected.

16 The Dante of Our Time

I have learned more from reading *The Gulag Archipelago* than from many erudite commentaries on totalitarian languages. I owe more to Solzhenitsyn than to most of the sociologists, historians, and philosophers who have been contemplating the fate of the West for the last thirty years. It is enigmatic that the publication of this work was enough to immediately shake our mental landscape and overturn our ideological guideposts.[1]

What exactly does it say that is so decisive, so staggering? We knew this truth; others had formulated it as far back as Koestler and Camus, Rousset and Merleau-Ponty. "Information" about the camps? The information was ours; we had the figures: occasionally approximations, but how much does a zero count when you are calculating in megadeaths! An unparalleled eyewitness account? But we knew it all, we had heard London, we had read Medvedev, the survivors had spoken, and their stories had been recorded. With Solzhenitsyn, then, and thanks to André Glucksmann, there was something else: an effect, a series of effects which were not simply a matter of "truth"; a work that did not aim to "teach" or deliver a "lesson." It is first of all *a work of art,* which, like all works of art, proves literally nothing, but bodies forth the unimaginable, gives a name to the unnamable, and above all forces us *to believe* what we were satisfied with *knowing.* Solzhenitsyn is the Shakespeare of our time, the only one capable of showing us the monsters and forcing us to see the horror and confront evil. He is our Dante as well, for he has the poet's fabulous power of creating images and myths for what by nature eludes analysis and conceptual form. We needed a *Divine Comedy* to represent Hell, the modern Hell of the Gulag, whose horrendous topography he has outlined in book after book.

Hence there was a chain reaction, first of all with reference to Marxism. All Solzhenitsyn had to do was *to speak* and we awoke from a dogmatic sleep. All he had to do was *to appear,* and an all too long history finally came to an end: the history of those Marxists who for thirty years had been retracing the path of decadence in search of their guilty party, moving painfully from the "bureaucratic phenomenon" to the "Stalinist deviation," from Stalin's "crimes" to Lenin's "mistakes," finally from Leninism to the blunders of the earliest apostles, going through the layers of the Marxian soil one by one, sacrificing a scapegoat at each stage, but always preserving above suspicion the one he dares to denounce for the first time—the founding father in person, Karl Kapital and his holy scriptures. This event was necessary in order for it to become possible to say to the dreamers of a golden age, to the unrepentant purists, that there was no vital spring of faith halfway down the slope, where nothing had been de-

cided, where everything was possible—the best as well as
the worst—in a dawning and primordial virginity, toward
which we were ordered to return every ten years. This
work was necessary in order for certain words to become
speakable, quite simply *speakable*—the words we had on
the tip of our tongues without daring to utter them, words
we intuited without knowing them or knew without
speaking them: there is no worm in the fruit, no late-
blooming sin, for the worm is the fruit and the sin is Marx.

Just think of the monumental deception we had lived
with for almost fifty years. If it was a matter of judging and
criticizing the principles of liberalism, there would never
be enough history, concrete and bloody history, to set in
opposition to them. The Declaration of the Rights of Man
was often judged by the standard of the massacre of the
Indians or the Le Chapelier law. No formal freedom could
stand up in the face of the scandal and the lie of its em-
bodiments. On the contrary, when Marxism-Leninism
was in question, a mysterious impunity seemed to preserve it. Some strange privilege maintained its dominance, and no argument from history was valid when
confronted with the learned authority of its doctrine. Two
weights and two measures. Truth in the West, falsehood
behind the iron curtain. Here, too, we needed Solzhenitsyn the *zek*, Solzehnitsyn the tramp, to set things straight,
to be able to proclaim what appears, once the book is
closed, to be obvious, so monumentally obvious that it is
astonishing we were able to ignore it for so long. The
Soviet camps are Marxist, as Marxist as Auschwitz was
Nazi. Marxism is not a science, but an ideology like the
others, operating like the others to conceal the truth at
the same time that it forms it. The horror is not a devia-

tion, a blemish, an abscess in the body of the proletarian State, but one effect among others of the laws of *Capital*. Why did it take us so long to read literally the doctrinal point that Beria had engraved on the gates of Kolyma?[2] Once again, we knew. All we had to do was to read.[3] The texts were available, and they said it clearly. We *knew* of the division that Marxism establishes between the competent on the one hand—history's officials, providence's confidants, the eternal heirs of Kautsky, who is the true *auctor* of the socialist State—and the ignorant on the other, playthings and marionettes, citizens of the darkness and cannon fodder, the infamous herd which, from Peter the Great to Stalin, has always bowed down in surrender. *It was impossible not to know* about the bloody knife which, from the *Manuscripts* to *Capital*, excludes the marginal, the declassed, the peasants, all those tramps, the mob which doctors Marx and Engels could not bear to have contaminating the radiant boulevards of the new world. We *knew* what line the barbed wire between classes passed through, not only, nor even essentially, between the bourgeoisie and its gravediggers, the supporters of the old and those of the new, but also, above all, between the latter and the scum, the lower orders, and the lumpenproletariat, who are something like their negative counterparts, the nothingness from which they have arisen. We knew, then, but we forgot, we refused or neglected to see. And here again, Solzhenitsyn has the virtue of *forcing us to look.* The strength of his text is that it forbids blindness. A luminous *Archipelago,* which proves in letters of blood that *Marxism is also a police force.*

And what police! What terror! What concern for order!

Have you ever seen police serving the cause of human "liberation"? Has there ever been an order which justified itself, with such vigor, on the basis of the necessity of a history and the truth of a dialectic? Vyshinsky and Bukharin had at least one point in common: they were Marxists; and consequently it was in the name of the same principles that the first accused and the second confessed. Princes had never discovered how to teach resignation and acceptance so effectively; between red power and its victims there is at least one point in common: the bond of iron and granite represented by the resigned, or passionate, attachment to the same body of principles. No imprisoned Marxist fails to believe in the deep, Marxist legitimacy of his imprisonment. There is no subjugated citizen whom the Marx-vigil does not remind that it is always right to give in. When you think of the wealth of casuistry the Church needed to justify the massacre of the Holy Innocents, when you remember the polemics about American intervention in Vietnam, you find yourself dreaming in the face of this prodigious discourse of voluntary servitude. You stand amazed in the face of this universal reason which never tires of defending the executioners against their victims.

Marx, then, the Machiavelli of the century. The U.S.S.R., or philosophy in power. It has been proved, in any case, that socialists are not only dreamers, gentle and tireless utopians, projecting into the heaven of ideas the sighs and torments of the humble and humiliated; but that Stalinism is a mode of socialism, socialism's mode of being, socialism as it is embodied in reality. That the classless society is not only an optimistic and messianic fantasy, unrealizable and inaccessible like all political dreams; but

that, on the contrary, it exists, it is another name for the
Terror, another name for the destruction of the kulaks,
the very real outcome of the unparalleled project of tearing a people from its moorings, its lineage, and its geography. That the Gulag is not a blunder or an accident, nut
a simple wound or aftereffect of Stalinism; but the necessary corollary of a socialism which can only actualize
homogeneity by driving the forces of heterogeneity back
to its fringes, which can aim for the universal only by
confining its rebels, its irreducible individualists, in the
outer darkness of a nonsociety. No camps without Marxism, said Glucksmann. We have to add: No socialism
without camps, *no classless society without its terrorist
truth.* [4]

Has the West heard the message? There aren't many of
us, in any case, who have listened to Solzhenitsyn. For the
moment, all eyes are rather directed toward Marx and
Stalin. Because finally, isn't this classless society bounded
by the hell of the concentration camps the practical realization of the oldest, most persistent project of the liberal
Prince? Can't we see in it clearly what he has been fanta-
sizing for two centuries but has not dared to push to its
limits—the state of Universality and the society of Uniformity? What is that socialism but the concrete proof that
the dream of leveling space and the social bond is not a
mad dream, that it can in fact come to pass? Kolyma is not
behind us like the distant vestige of rudimentary repression; it is perhaps before us, like a terrible premonition of
barbaric desocialization and the conditions that make it
possible.[5] Stalinism is not dead and buried in the bad
conscience of its unfrocked disciples; perhaps it repre-

sents the horizon of the uprooted, abstract, and equalized humanity which the smiling Princes would like to make into the material of their power. Beware Stalinism with a human face, which might well have the body of what we recently still called societies of freedom, a body which is today taking on the form of a vigorous "technocracy."

17 The Proletarian Age

If all this is correct, we have to draw certain concrete and precise conclusions. First of all, our sociologists, political scientists, and futurologists are generally on the wrong track when they depict the future of industrial society. What exactly do they say? That we are heading directly toward a world of "white-collar" workers, "technicians," and a "service" economy. That the West of tomorrow will be populated by bankers, stockholders, and civil servants. That this is the necessary consequence of the gradual disappearance of the working class, overcome by the pressures of progress and automation. That there is already dominant everywhere a "petty bourgeoisie" whose outlines are badly defined, whose status is vague and indefinite, and which is talked about all the more because no one has anything precise to say about it. Everyone is complicit in this process, modernist technocrats as well as the most subtle Marxists, leftists who have settled down and sociologists of work, the prophets of the postindustrial age and the apostles of the middle classes: the disciples of Aron, Fourastié, and Touraine all mixed together, Poulantzas along with Mallet, Reynaud, and Duvignaud. And even Deleuze and Guattari lend their support to the refrain when they declare, in *Anti-Oedipus,* that there is now only one real class under capitalist rule and that class is the bourgeoisie. This is a well-known tune, then, too familiar, trite. I would like to argue against it the directly contrary thesis that there will in fact be only one class in the coming barbarism, but that class no doubt will be, against all expectations, the working class, or if you prefer, the proletariat.

A paradox? I think not. And I even see it rather as the necessary conclusion to everything I have attempted to say about barbarian "technology." It is especially one of the conclusions of the theoretical work of serious German philosophy between the wars, those Heideggerian or para-Heideggerian texts on which I have relied several times. For they raise, in an exemplary way, the question not only of the fate of the West but of its very being as an object and as an object of thought. I am referring to *Holzwege,* the *Letter* and *Being and Time*; but also to the accursed author of *Total Mobilization,*[6] the thinker with suspect descendants—that Niekrisch[7] was his disciple can never exonerate him for the crime of having produced Rauschnig[8]—to Ernst Jünger, whom one day, in spite of everything, we will have to bring ourselves to reread. Why? Because he clearly sets out, fifty years in advance, a theoretical description of what the modern world holds in store: the "historic" effect of the "endless winter," the "night of the world" presaged by the triumph of technology; the peculiar landscape of a universal that has become worldwide through the combined obstinacy of capital and its shadow, the socialist tradition.

What in fact is meant by "total mobilization"? It is of

course the essence of the butchery of 1914–1918, but also, in a deeper sense, the advent of an unparalleled figure on the surface of the planet and the generalization in all corners of the world of a "style" unknown to any previous civilization: the figure of the *worker* as the style and fate of man, contemporary nihilistic man. Jünger says roughly that work is no longer the lot of the wretched alone: It has become the lot of the earth itself in its intimate relationship to us, the ones who shape it. It is no longer the fate held in store for the humiliated, the exploited, and the oppressed: It is the burden of a liturgy for which socialists and capitalists, by the same right and in the same way, are priests and acolytes. There is no region of being that escapes from its law, no individual who does not bow to its command, and no social group which does not share the same daily bread. To be sure, the class struggle persists, and it continues to set the tempo for industrial cacophony. This is probable, even certain, empirically obvious. But this struggle is entirely set to a single melody tirelessly repeated by Marxist historicism and by bourgeois economism, each in its own register: the harsh and monotonous song of the "worker" style in which the particularities of the past have finally found their miraculous melting pot.

Nietzsche already had this intuition, in a fragment of *The Will to Power,* in which he foresaw a "pale race of liberals" who would combine the attributes of the slaves and the "superfluous men" of the past; and his only mistake was to paint it with the colors of "finance" and "trade."[9] It was Bataille's intuition when he diagnosed modern neglect of the insignia of expenditure as the dawn of a world without sovereignty, with the reservation that he at least continued to see class struggle as "a superior form of potlatch."[10] Closer to us, there is Klossowski, who describes (referring, in fact, to Nietzsche) a universe in which masters will no longer be masters, nor slaves slaves either; in which all will be uniformly mingled in the "eternal necessity" of a "fermentation" devoid of sense—and devoid of the sense of power;[11] but he, too, makes the mistake of not seeing in that condition the mark of the most implacable form of domination ever invented by the West. For the truth that lies in these notions of the pale race of liberals, power stripped of its sovereignty, and generalized servitude, must be pushed still further. This uniformity in the middle and equilibrium in the shallows have to be thought through to their deepest foundations. Not as the advent of a pseudo "new class," with everyone communicating through the same dismal mediocrity. Not as the degenerate form of the ancient confrontation of wolf with wolf. Nor finally as the "acephalic" disappearance of force and constraint considered as the only or principal attributes of power. But much more as the absolutely unparalleled form of a proletarian barbarism, as an illustration of the thesis in which I am tempted to see the principle for understanding contemporary nihilism: The proletariat is the class which fails to give birth to the good society, but succeeds, on the contrary, by consecrating the barbarian state.

Thus I have to specify and refine what I asserted earlier. An "impossible class," I said, meaning the impossibility of a "class," of an antagonistic pole, undermining by its negativity the equilibrium of the social body. And in saying that I was attempting to track down historical optimism in its most solid political fortress. But now I add that it is possible, a very possible "style," understood not as a negative but as a positive entity, not as a limb but as the entire body, not as an "adversary ideal" but as the language and character of the modern world and the modern age—and here I am simply carrying the hypothesis of pessimism to its logical conclusion. I also said that the proletariat does not and cannot have the political unity attributed to it by the faithful, it is a nothingness of identity, an absence of difference, an indiscernible whole. But now I say that confusion does not exclude homogeneity, uniformity in nothingness, a flat and nameless surface— and the first is even a precondition for the second. I maintained that every revolution in this century was a bourgeois revolution, that 1871, 1917, and 1949 can all be reduced to the historical model set up in 1789. But the paradox works both ways, and it can just as well be maintained that there has never been a bourgeoisie which ruled specifically and in person, which did not dominate through absence and withdrawal—in other words, every modern revolution was plebeian and working class in the broad sense of the term. The proletariat is the only class that can't be seen? To be sure, but that is proof less of its disappearance than of its omnipresence. It is without culture but present everywhere in culture, without collective representation but present everywhere in the collective imagination. The ruling ideology, to parody the Marxists, is turning out to be the ideology of the ruled class.

You ask for proofs? I will offer one shortly with respect to Marxism, recently elevated to the status of hegemonic culture in Western societies. For the moment, here are a few symptoms as signs and points of reference. The persistence, for example, of political subjects as worn out and especially as lacking in credibility as *nationalization*. The return of those old mirages which come to us from the very beginnings of modernity, but which everyone, on the right as well as the left, thinks it right and proper to make into his banner: shareholding, participation, *self-management*. The new strength of the quasi-feudal powers, the genuine "privileges" represented by the *unions*. The strange and paradoxical vitality of those fossilized parties whose decline is periodically announced without ever taking place: the Stalinist parties. Where have they been seen declining? They have never been so powerful nor so close to exercising power. Where have they been seen running out of steam? They maintain better than ever their famous dual language: adherence in principle to the "alternation" of power on one hand, and on the other the stubborn belief in a socialism that will be irreversible once the process is set in motion. A contradiction? Rather a penetrating, very penetrating insight into the foreseeable development of capitalist mechanisms. George Orwell predicted a proletarian future in which the workers would be the slaves; Georges Marchais, for his part, is betting on a proletarian future of which they will be the masters and the great organizers. The proletariat, the final avatar of the declining bourgeoisie.

Today the "dangerous classes" hardly exist any more, and no one any longer believes seriously in the threat they represent. They are simply in the process of occupying the heart and the throne of the mechanisms of production. The "postindustrial" age that reformers constantly din into our ears is the drunkenness of technology and the religion of management: its priests will one day be the immediate agents of the technological process, the working classes. The communist menace? It is called Eurocommunism, socialism with a human face, power to the workers: everything seems to point to the rightness of the Western C.P.s' obstinacy. Capitalism? I have said that it is not about to die down and waste away, it is not even as far from the economic analyses of *Capital* as one may think: but with the reservation that its wretched are no longer the excluded. For, prophecy for prophecy, here is what my crystal ball predicts: a capitalism which is no longer heads, a proletariat no longer tails, a proletarian capitalism, a capitalist proletariat, a mode of production which, without ever ceasing to be what Marx said it was, is from this point on entirely impregnated with proletarian values and images.

This idea was, by the way, not foreign to Marx himself. He saw it as one of the possible futures of capital. In the *Economic and Philosophic Manuscripts* there is a little-known passage which develops precisely this notion. The passage mentions a mode of production about which, as far as I know, he later said practically nothing, and it is difficult to integrate it into the classic pattern. He mentions a mode of production which he calls "crude and unthinking communism."[12] Why "communism"? Because it abolishes private property and thereby abolishes class distinctions. Why "crude and unthinking"? Because it abolishes property only by generalizing it, and it abolishes class distinctions by extending the condition of the worker to all men. "The community," says Marx, "is simply a community of labor and equality of wages, which are paid out by the communal capital, the community as universal capitalist." This is indeed a kind of socialism, since the class struggle has disappeared and the social

sphere is unified. And yet it still contains a kind of capitalism, communal and universal, no doubt, but capitalist all
the same, since capital continues to exist. It is also a
"proletarian" regime, since wage labor has become the
common fate; but it is still nevertheless a "bourgeois"
regime, since capital has only been divided or made uniform, which in fact amounts to the same thing—the same-
ness of its permanence. Can it be said that the proletarian
no longer exists because the bond of exploitation is no
longer clearly visible in a labor contract? He exists more
than ever, since he no longer needs a contract to devote
his life to labor. Can it be said that there is no question of
a proletariat because it no longer confronts an antagonistic force? It's a matter of definition, but in any case it's
proof that the proletariat is in the process of becoming the
new master of the earth. "Crude and unthinking communism" is the same old economism crossed with socialist
humanism. It is the Marxian prophecy of the dual
hegemony I alluded to at the beginning of this chapter.

18 Marxism: The Opium of the People

This proletarian age needed a new sphere, a new cultural space. This new barbarism needed a religion, some kind of social bond. And indeed it seems that the consecrated texts of materialism have fulfilled the old function, and that *Capital* represents modern canon law. Marxism is the religion of our time, and as we shall see, this has to be understood literally.

You won't find in these pages the weak and muddled banalities usually set forth on this subject. For example, it hardly matters that the materialist texts function like a bible, as subjects of commentary and grounds for judging heresies. For after all, it is the fate of any theoretical system to approach theology and drift into scholasticism: Good Aristotles are worth more than epigones of Nietzsche. It also hardly matters that Marxist parties operate like churches, rediscovering their liturgies and reproducing their rituals, that they are counter-societies confined to the rarefied atmosphere of hierarchies from another age. For my part, I see in this the sign of the grand style which creates a politics, and I prefer, all things considered, democratic centralism to the cloudy liberalism of democratic business culture. I am also quite ready to agree that communist militants are secular priests, as everybody keeps telling us these days, that the energy that drives them is the energy of the ascetic and the hermit, that they are possessed by the paranoid rage to represent and dispense justice. But isn't that precisely their grandeur, a final trace of nobility in a universe without sovereignty? So, long live the ascetic ideal as an ethical exercise! Long live the militant ideal for its idiosyncratic style! The world would be better if we were still pious.

In other words, the problem doesn't lie there and I'm aiming at something entirely different when I take up the old complaint. That isn't the problem, and the question has to be dealt with in a much more radical way. Perhaps we should reread Augustine, who dared to say in the *Retractiones* that Christendom is not in Christendom, that it has not always been and no doubt will not always be the Christendom we know, that it comes to us from much further back, from an immemorial source, from the deepest and most secret of the living springs of paganism. We should reread Nietzsche too, the Nietzsche of *The Dawn* and the posthumous fragments, who showed the survival as well as the preexistence of Christendom, that it continues as a form, a culture, and a social bond well beyond the time of its extinction—that it is endlessly coming to an end, dying, and being reborn in the interminable stream of its secular and socialist incarnations. And we should reread Marx above all, yes, the Marx of the *Critique of Hegel's Philosophy of Right*, who himself perhaps reveals, unknowingly and against all expectations, the key to the whole question. Everyone knows the passage in which, while stigmatizing religion as a school of resignation and training for acceptance—the famous "opium of the people"—he simultaneously offers to it, and this is often forgotten, the most stirring tribute: "the sigh of the oppressed creature." I propose simply to comment on this passage. This is the passage I would like to reread or, more precisely, rewrite: substituting "Marxism" wherever he says "religion"; analyzing it in detail in order to turn it against its author. And it will clearly appear that it is not enough to say that Marxism is a caricature of Christianity. Marxism, more fundamentally, has become Christianity's current stand-in, taking on, for better or worse, the entire scope of its vocation.*

"Religion," says Marx, "is the general theory of this world." But Marxism is precisely that, and it provides concrete proof of this fact every day. It is a masterful theory of the accumulation of capital, an impeccable instrument for the analysis of the contradictions of liberalism, and it is particularly irreplaceable for anyone who wants to periodize history and march in step with it, but it long ago fell into the public domain and is undisputed by experts of every description and politicians of every stripe. Who on the left, among the economists who call themselves Marxists, is willing to remember, except de-

---

*"Religion is the general theory of this world, its encyclopedic compendium, its logic in popular form, its spiritual *point d'honneur*, its enthusiasm, its moral sanction, its solemn complement, and its universal basis of consolation and justification. . . . The struggle against religion is therefore indirectly the struggle against that world whose spiritual aroma is religion.

"Religious suffering is at one and the same time the expression of real suffering and a protest against real suffering. Religion is the sigh of the oppressed creature, the heart of a heartless world and the soul of a soulless condition. It is the opium of the people."

ceitfully or following convention, that Marxism originally presented itself as a weapon of political struggle, a battering ram against the Princes, a banner to give men the daring to struggle and overthrow the collective superego which prohibited rebellion? Raised to the dignity of science, an objective and sterilized science, no longer true because it is effective, but effective because it is true, the identity of its proponents is no longer important; it is used as a tool, a grid to articulate and appropriate some "raw" reality. Who on the right, among its most subtle official opponents, maintains the distrust, the *cordon sanitaire,* of the past? Where is the Keynesian who does not find comfort in Marxism, who fails to use it to complete his arsenal? Marxism in these hands has become a formidable mechanism for thinking about "investment," predicting "reconstruction," and struggling against "inflation."[13] We have financial officials who, without saying so, obviously resort to it as much for day-to-day management as during periods of serious crisis.[14] And I am familiar with businessmen's journals which have no hesitation in mobilizing substantial Marxist training in order to justify their choices and their political bets. In the end, Bernstein was right to predict that materialism would have the future of bourgeois illusions. And Breton was particularly perceptive when, in 1936, he stigmatized its "weary abandonment to wonder at what exists." Fact-worshipping, pragmatic, realistic, and at the service of *Realpolitik,* Marxism is in the process of becoming the modern form of the consensus through which the republic of the wise and learned have always established their communion. It is no longer, if it ever was, the theory of revolutions that shatter the course of events, but more and more the interpreter, often masterful, of the weighty continuities that make for its permanence.

This is why the formulation "encyclopedic compendium" also suits it so well, as an adequate expression of its new-found imperialism. The time is past when it rejected psychoanalysis, consigned it without comment to the outer darkness of ideology. A year does not go by without the appearance of weighty and very serious "contributions" to a Marxist "treatment" of the Freudian epistemological break.[15] The time is also long past when it considered only popular and proletarian literature, paying furtive and almost clandestine attention to the other kind. Modern Marxists theorize about "literary production,"[16] and this no longer ends at the borders of "bourgeois" taste. If the Lysenko affair is indeed closed, if, as we are assured, a new affair of the kind is unthinkable, this is not because the communists have abjured their old demons, nor because liberal reason has conquered their Stalinist madness. In fact, the opposite is true: They have internalized Lysenkoism by standing it on its feet, they have made its excesses commonplace by criticizing its deviations, and they now settle questions in biology and contribute to physics quietly and without scandal; and general indifference greeted Dominique Lecourt's[17] proposal of the "theses about knowledge" which the new ideologues have placed at the service of scientists. We have a Marxist urbanism, a Marxist psychoanalysis, a Marxist aesthetic, a Marxist numismatics.[18] There is no longer any realm of knowledge that Marxism fails to have a look at, no area off limits, no taboo territory. There are no cultural fronts to which it fails to send cohorts of researchers with the mission to "intervene," as the jargon would have it. And by

the way, this is doubtless the deep meaning of Althusserism and the reason for its success: an unprecedented effort
to extend theory to all the continents that had resisted it
up to that point, to penetrate into every area of the encyclopedia.

"General theory and encyclopedic compendium" of
this world, Marxism is through and through "its logic in a
popular form." For here, too, the heirs of *Capital* have
perpetuated the division, on which Christendom based its
existence, between the commentary of scholars, erudite
and refined, and coarser and more simplified Church
Latin. They illustrate the absolute rule of the history of
ideas according to which scientism and encyclopedism
are the founders of koine, a common language, a vulgate.
There is not *one* history of materialism, but two connected though relatively autonomous histories.[19] On the
one hand, there is an elite Marxism, created by elites and
addressed to them, which every generation puts back on
the drawing board, claiming to return to its origins. On
the other, there is a Marxism for the masses, again created
by elites, but addressed to militants, a sonorous vade
mecum broadcast by the apparatus. It is not an accident
that Louis Althusser, one of the most brilliant Marxist
theoreticians of the century, in any case one of those who
carried out the demand for rigor to the greatest extent, is
the contemporary, and not only in a temporal sense, of a
communist party which will survive in history as the in-
ventor of the pitiful concepts of historic bloc[20] and "mo-
nopoly state capitalism." Moreover, to the same Althusser, speaking of "Ideological State Apparatuses"
controlled by the bourgeoisie and charged with making
certain that its vision of the world is propagated, one

could retort that Marxist parties, too, have their apparatuses, and much more effective ones at that, since they are today propagating the new "popular logic" of capital, a stock of banalities and commandments which have taken the place of those of yesterday's Prince, and they nourish that logic with new mythologies.

For, and in this it continues to resemble religion, Marxism tends to become this very world's "spiritualist *point d'honneur,* its enthusiasm, its moral sanction, [and] its solemn complement." In this case, experience needs no commentary; it is a flagrant presence at our doorstep and in our memory: the experience of the Stalinist trials, for which vulgar or sophisticated Marxism served as a mask or a justification—as a "spiritualist *point d'honneur"*—for the executioners; the attitude of the condemned, transfixed, enchanted, petrified, and somehow *fired* by their own principles, which were the very ones that simultaneously condemned them; the example of the Soviet death camps, openly and explicitly sanctioned by materialism, an orthodox materialism that operated completely as an alibi for them and therefore as their "moral sanction." Still closer to us is the example of the liberal head of state[21] who believes it appropriate to decorate his speech with delicate references to a dogmatic system with whose mechanisms he apparently lacks familiarity, but about which he knows very well that it can be the "solemn complement" that demonstrates the excellence and the good will of a banal or cynical proposal. Our masters have no more "heart" than does the world they govern, and the heart they borrowed in the past from religion they now seek in the company of religion's nemesis. The Princes have no more "spirit" than the history which carries them; they used to derive this spirit from providence, but now it comes from Marxism—the most formidably ordered system of thought the West has ever invented.

This is all the more true because it is also, for the oppressed, a "universal basis of consolation and justification." Christianity consoled by a promised paradise: Though you have suffered here, you will experience bliss in the beyond. Marxism also consoles, but in the name of the dialectic: For the moment you are a slave, but tomorrow you will be a dictator. Christianity justified the world by proving its harmony: Evil is the shadow of good, the contingent form of the divine plan. Marxism justifies the world in its own way, by certifying the Enlightenment: Evil is a stage toward good, a provisional form of human progress. I have already said that socialism, far from ordering rebellion, preaches resignation because it sanctifies the order of being and recognizes decline only as a detour in the procession. The Marxism that is the basis of socialism is similarly a thought of peace, a declaration of peace on earth, because it believes in a history to which it attributes a movement toward an end, because it recognizes the existence of war but denies its necessity, because it believes, in a word, in the tortuous, but in the end ineluctable, advent of the good society. Thus, if Marx was right to say that the "struggle against religion is . . . indirectly the struggle against that world whose spiritual aroma is religion," the formulation can once again be reversed and the parallel pursued with impeccable rigor: The struggle against Marxism is indeed, indirectly, the struggle against that world of which it is not only the spiritual aroma, but also the most subtle and cunning consecration.

As for the end of the passage, the tribute offered to

religion, "the sigh of the oppressed creature," and simultaneously "the opium of the people," the parallel still
holds. In fact, Marxism, too, can express protest against
"the real crisis," while simultaneously elsewhere induc-
ing or provoking it. It, too, expresses that sigh, while at
the same time making itself into a mere interpreter of
oppression, incapable of doing anything to remedy it.
You may denounce it and demystify it as much as you
like; there is at least one thing you cannot take away
from it: its capacity to sustain parties and patterns of
thought that I would not call revolutionary, but simply
"popular." You can refuse to recognize the patents on
subversion it unwarrantedly grants itself, but there is at
least one claim to virtue it has not usurped: It is able to
embody, under particular conditions, the resistance of
the "little people" against the power of the "great," the
protest of peoples against the excesses of Princes. I am
deliberately using the vocabulary of *poujadisme.* For
this, and nothing but this, is Marxism's virtue: It provides
a contemporary form of the old, very old, function of the
regulation of disputes that the ancients called the "trib-
une's power." I maintain, of course, that the Marxist parties are the bemused worshippers of the order of what
exists: but nevertheless, within this order, in the West at
least, they are sometimes the only ones who express,
without deception or disguise, the interests of the impoverished. No one can deny their incapacity to give
birth to any variety of rebellious thought, but that does
not exclude the possibility that "some" rebellion can
come through that very incapacity. It is a *reactionary*
system of thought, then, but this is to be understood in
the strictest sense: a reaction to the threat of revolution,

of course, but also a reaction to the oppressive rigor of the law.

In this sense, and only in this sense, we can accept the cliché of the "Communist Church." Indeed, confronted with this belief in order which paradoxically claims to take sides with the humiliated, confronted with this repressive discourse which in fact finds its supporters in the plebeian layers of society, how is it possible not to think of the famous statement in St. Matthew, the involuntary ancestor of "historic compromises": Render unto Caesar the things which are Caesar's: worldly power and authority over the body; and unto God the things that are God's: faith in the beyond and the direction of the soul. Confronted with these authoritarian parties, methodically purged of their dissidents of every kind, those interfering and unrepentant madmen of the revolution, how is it possible not to think of the division instituted by triumphant Christendom between the service of the Prince, which requires a homogeneous community purged of God's fools, and the service of the people, which consists simply of listening to their pious sighs, their complaints, and their sorrows, only to transform them into the radiant language of eschatological messianism? What could Pope Paul VI and the communist mayor of Rome have possibly said to one another when they met at the end of 1976?[22] Spiritual *points d'honneur* of a disintegrating power, men of heart deprived of guarantees and alibis, did they envisage a new concordat, this time not between Church and State, but between Church and party? One thing is certain: As I write this, Rome is in the process of becoming *the capital of the West.* The eternal city of both Christendom and Marxism, it is very precisely the site of their historic compromise. *Pax Romana* once again, between the eternal Prince and the future Prince of this world.

19 May 1968, or the Defeat of Life

Concretely, this means that the question of Marxism, which has troubled us so much during the last ten years, is perhaps not as simple as some people believed and as I myself thought for a long time. That it is not saying enough to proclaim oneself anti-Marxist, even from the left or from a quasi-Maoist position. That we have to reevaluate the importance and the meaning of the debate, and guard against the crass optimism of "We've won" and the facile atheism whose subtle tricks are only too familiar. Marxism is the religion of this time? A certain number of consequences flow from this, and I would like, very briefly, to bring out the connections between them.

First of all: Against all expectations, in spite of our vows and our obstinate denials, Marxism is healthy, has never been so healthy. The crisis of Marxism exists only in our minds and in our books. I said that its fate will resemble the past fate of Christianity, that it will impregnate, in spite of its intellectual decline, every stratum, every pore of civil and political society. I might even say, speaking metaphorically, that it also operates like another, more familiar ideology, the ideology of Radicalism between the wars. Remember: the Radical theoreticians had grown sterile long before the France of postmen, elementary school teachers, and the middle classes had become followers of Bouglé, Alain and Ravaisson. The France that was thinking was Breton, Malraux, or Aragon, and even Drieu, who saw things clearly in *Gilles* when he described a France truly radicalized in the depths of its daily life and in its fantasies. The great debates of the time were between surrealism and revolution, communism and the Spanish Civil War, rebellion and literature, while the deep layers of the country were still deciding about the conflict between Church and State, between Combes and the monastic orders, between pacifism and the war effort. The naïveté of the avant-garde, the impudence of the forerunners! Marxism–Leninism is the *radicalisme* of our time. Modern France produces materialism as Monsieur Jourdain produced prose. Tomorrow it will be, perhaps it already is, Marxified beyond the dreams of the learned and the master thinkers.

This Marxism is of course not written down in books or learned treatises. It is contained in a few simple formulas, in a finite collection of clichés which suffice to create a mosaic of the spirit of the age. It is what makes the socialists say that Valéry Giscard d'Estaing is a "representative of big capital." It is what inspires so many futile and banal analyses of the two or three "fractions" of the bourgeoisie struggling for power and, as they say, hegemony. This Marxism is what one finds everywhere in the universities, the media, or party leaderships, in the new conditioned reflexes of the "socialist" managers of so-called bourgeois society. At the moment when the choice was between de Gaulle and Pétain, popular France was still mulling over its memories of the Marne and Verdun. When the fight was between Chaban-Delmas and Giscard d'Estaing, it was still settling accounts between Pétainism and the resistance. How could it be otherwise in the close hothouse atmosphere of the history of ideas and ideologies? How will a book like this one be read while everyone is expatiating about Eurocommunism, the crisis of the state, or the political evolution of Althusser? Marxism is more than ever the central question of the day: Sartre did not know how right he was to assert that it was "unavoidable." We need an archaeology of the present time that would be able to discover the traces of Marxism in the tight patterns that regulate the shape of our discourse and govern the ways in which it is propagated.

Can it be said that this Marxism is not really Marxism, on the pretext that it circulates, as though it were a gas, through texts that make no reference to it and among people who are ignorant of it? In a sense, this is true, but it is also true that every great system of thought is illiterate, that a text isn't worth anything until the ignorant appropriate it, and that you don't need to read in order to recite, nor even to recite in order to be, much less know something in order to understand it. The West was Christian even when the Scriptures were not read in the countryside. The Greek world was Homeric even if, outside the Mycenaean palaces, the *Iliad* and the *Odyssey* were literally dead letters. In fact, we have to stop judging the importance of a system of thought according to the noise its heralds make or the work of its commentators. We have to sharpen our hearing enough to be able to hear another noise, the scarcely audible murmur from the chorus of imitators and ventriloquists' dummies. We have to be bold enough to say of *Anti-Oedipus,* for example, that it is less important at Vincennes or through learned interpretations than in and through the effects produced by untutored readings and plagiarisms. When will there be horsemen of the intellect who will dare to proclaim that Deleuze represents the spontaneously deadly thought of every kind of depravity? When will we have an elementary anti-Marxism that will say that the left, which extends to the reformist right, is materialist, materialist from top to bottom, even if it understands nothing—in fact, because it understands nothing—about the uniqueness of the Marxian epistemological break?

The second consequence is that although, in the face of this frozen horizon, there have indeed been attempts at a thaw and a critique of Marxism, paradoxically this critique has so far failed to create a crisis of Marxism, but has rather increased its strength and hardened its positions. I say this with some bitterness, for I am not entirely outside the movement and I have been a kind of sponsor, at least through publicity and editorial judgment. But the facts are there, the distressing series of commentaries that greeted Benoist and Dollé, Lardreau, Jambet, and Françoise Paul-Lévy. There is a painful distance, a mysterious gap, between the philosophical and the strictly political effects of their works. There is a strange discrepancy between the public that has been reached and the one that was addressed, and some have had to pay a heavy price for this. I know these books are read, but I also know they carry no weight; they are foreign bodies for the official left, transplants that cannot be assimilated by its established institutions. I know their authors are celebrated, but rather as new monsters of the historical unconscious, "new gurus," than as sorcerers; more honored than excluded, praised and sometimes embalmed. I don't think Glucksmann has persuaded anyone on the left, and not a single Marxist has been shaken by *Marx est mort.* This is a common occurrence in the history of ideas: Many significant ideas were rejected or ignored in their age, and always as a direct result of their critical and subversive force. The "new philosophers," since this is what they are called, have been misunderstood, incorrectly interpreted, and badly read. How could it be otherwise with a somnambulistic and somehow stupefied left which is still rehearsing obscure debates about reform and revolution, and whose theoretical spectrum has not got beyond the sour polemics of Lenin and Hilferding?

This is why we have to get rid of the foolish commonplace that May 1968 was the beginning of an era of intellectual thaw and the subversion of orthodoxies. Exactly the opposite happened, and I offer as proof—it is not the only one—the recent evolution of the largest party in France, the new claimant to the throne: the Socialist party. Is it not in fact disturbing to see it choose precisely this moment, the post-May period of "angelism" and anti-Marxism, to discover a doctrine it had ignored in the past with such pride and dignity. What are we to think of the newly knowledgeable ideologues who recite to militants curious litanies that we thought had been consigned forever to the museum of theoretical horrors? Doesn't it seem like a dream when we see them, after a delay of ten years, exhume our own dogmas and cheerfully parade in clothes which they believe to be new but which are as old

as our disillusionments? Journals are published in which—
without, by the way, any changes from the prudent refor-
mism of the past—the great theses of *Capital* are subjected to vigorous and detailed analysis. A little class analysis, a hint of infrastructure, a dialectical subtlety, and the
trick is played and respectability assured! A commentary
on Althusser, a kick in the pants for Garaudy,[23] and respectability becomes acumen, the result is guaranteed
and the proof invulnerable. A preface to Gramsci, a little
voyage through Italian Marxism, and there you have it,
the Lenin of the West adding spice to the social-medio-
cratic gruel.

For the inescapable fact is that May 1968 was not only
the libertarian explosion described by so many nostalgic
orphans. Nor was it only the beginning of a slow drift that
has gradually brought so many Stalinoid leftists to break
with Marxism. It was that, of course, it was that *too*, and
it would even be *essentially* that if one chose to take the
point of view of eternity on the phenomenon. But as for
the present, this present that threatens to last and to ex-
pand for a long time, exactly the opposite is true. May
1968 is one of the darkest dates in the history of socialism;
the moment of truth for a tradition which neither Herr,
nor Pivert, nor Frossard, nor Guesde had succeeded in
converting; the point of reversal for an ideological line
which nothing and no one had been able to divert from
an amiable liberalism skilled in stealing what it needed
wherever it could. The uprising was necessary in order for
half of France to recognize itself in a party which speaks
the language of the communists even if it does not resemble them, which believes it to be just and proper to speak
that language and no other at the risk of spreading fear

and reviving the old scarecrows. The "revolution" of May was necessary to make the new Prince feel obliged to adopt the Marxism without which he no doubt imagines he cannot take or maintain power. There has been too much talk, after all, about the "co-opting" of the victories of 1968: The "bourgeoisie" co-opted nothing at all; it was satisfied to step over the phenomenon and finally rally behind its most faithful prophets.

On the other hand, the third consequence is that this rediscovered Marxism has lost its fruitfulness, that vivified by its new vocation, it has paradoxically settled into a strange torpor. Yes, it has become a kind of encyclopedia; but what absence of thought, what conceptual poverty! Yes, it is the "general theory" of our world; but this world, in its theory, appears entirely made up of banality, a pure and simple reproduction of the technocratic universe. I know very well that there was Althusser, who was certainly much more distinguished and who carried theoretical rigor to a very high level. But Althusserism died out with the Maoist explosion in France, and it rapidly declined as the post-May period wound down the turns of its spiral. Someday we'll need to explain what *For Marx* and *Reading Capital* meant for the generation of intellectuals who were twenty in the sixties—harsh and haughty books which forged their concepts as you hammer out slogans, which made words resonate like banners flapping in the wind, which unfurled their logic as you set out a battle plan; and the style, especially the style, redundant and triumphal, allusive and programmatic, operated all by itself like a prodigious machine for mobilizing the will to know and the desire to be a militant. Theorize, it said: The revolution comes at that price. As for me, at any rate, I came very close to owing him *everything*.

His was a strange adventure, this communist who, buried in his office on the rue d'Ulm, where he was established like a new Lucien Herr, unknowingly, or at least *unwillingly*, unleashed the most formidable anticommunist offensive the left has ever known. It was a disturbing odyssey for this professor who, at the moment when the good news of the red guards arrived from China, was teaching Marxist students the rudiments of a Maoism which would later prove the source of an unprecedented break with the tradition. This history which is his, and which is also ours, is above all the history of a failure, a theoretical and political bankruptcy which a number of us lived through painfully. For Althusser quickly disappeared, as quickly as he had come, forced to retreat to an attentive and bitter silence, turning into a Feuerbach, of whom we were the illegitimate offspring.[24] The old party was still there, and it welcomed him with open arms, all too happy to find again the most prodigal of its children, and perhaps also in too much of a hurry to remove from his now impassive and silent face the stigmata of his escapade. Elevated to the rank of counselor to the heirs to the throne, Louis Althusser then fell into an indolent lethargy; and thus came to an end, in the obscure backwater of sterile "self-criticism," Marxism's last chance, the final attempt to restore to it the polish and the brilliance of the past.

To tell the truth, I have become aware in the very process of writing that this is not exactly the way the problem ought to be raised nor the way history should be written. In fact, Althusser was not Marxism's last chance, he was its desperado, and he was a desperado because there was no hope at all. Here again, we have to go back in time: from the moment that Marxism became a vulgate, no Althusser in the world could do anything against the law that makes the vulgates of every age into soft underbellies of theory incapable of creating or even absorbing what is new. As soon as Marxism became a koine, it lost in understanding what it gained in extension, and it paid for its expansion with total sterility. The phenomenon is well known, and historical illustrations of it are not lacking. The decline of the Roman Empire began precisely at the moment when Latin functioned as the common language of the peoples it had conquered. The death of the Hellenic world was also contemporaneous with the apogee of the Hellenistic koine, a common and economical language which had lost the beautiful extravagance of the language of Sophocles and Aeschylus. The Church was always most alive, intellectually most vigorous, during the periods when it was most divided—the Reformation, of course, the liberalization of the nineteenth century, the Marxizing of Catholicism today.[25] These examples are there to show that a common language means the death of discourse, that once we hear each other we no longer understand, once we eliminate noise we can no longer hear anything, and that by the same token, Marxism is, simultaneously and without contradiction, the thought of our century and the obstacle to its thought.

A fourth and final consequence: If all the preceding is correct, then it means that anti-Marxism is at one and the same time an impossible and a necessary position. What critique can stand up in the face of the infinite power of this religion of modern times? The perennial anathematizers of deviations and betrayals are not very credible. In such matters, there is nothing less treacherous than a deviation or more orthodox than a heresy, for, *pace* the Trotskyites, Stalin was above all a dogmatist—that is, faithful, excessively faithful, to the original vulgate. Those who are nostalgic for the other road, I mean the libertarian road, forget that there is not, not any longer, any room for that kind of socialism inside the solidified world of Marxism. It is not an accident, for example, that the "self-management" that comes to us directly from Charles Gide and Fauquet is still, after eight years of debate, a flat and empty formula. Shall we embark on a critique in the holy name of history? If we are talking about accomplished history, the Marxists are always right, and if we are talking about future history, it has no better oracles. In the name of desire and the ebbs and flows of pleasure? I have shown how the Deleuzeans unknowingly reproduce the essential aspects of the materialist schema. In the name of Foucault's micropowers? I believe that they are unthinkable without the support of new universals which do not, to our distress, have the logical force of the universals of *Capital*.[26] Whatever angle you choose, the citadel is unassailable. And we have to say of Marxism everything, neither more nor less, that I said of the Master.

No more: This means that it is not in the long run susceptible to particular treatment, that there is not, properly speaking, a "question" of Marxism as such, and that anti-Marxism must not become a religion reproducing the fanaticism it claims to combat. No less: This means in turn that there is nothing said about the Master in general that cannot also be said about this particular master, that there is no argument pertinent to one that is not pertinent to the other, and that the problem of Marxism has become a representative case, the most pressing and contemporary of representative cases, of the eternal problem of misery and submission. Thus, in reality, the only point of view that holds up and does not get bogged down in the swamps of agnosticism is the one that has always stood up against this image of misery: the point of view of rebellion and the wager on a world without a master. Anti-Marxist? Yes, that is what we must be, and it means two things: first, that—powerless to think of revolution without reducing it to schemata that stifle its explosive originality, incapable, for example, of thinking about the great medieval rebellions[27] without seeing them simply as an "anticipation" of communist politics, a mixture of "archaic vestiges" and "proletarian possibilities," the ghostly "prophecy" of an end of history that has always been already given—Marxism is, literally, counterrevolutionary thought; and, second, that if thereby the question of revolution can once more have a meaning, if the mad project to change one's life and to change the world can today have some basis, if the West needs new reasons to struggle and new buttresses for the foolishness of rebellion, then, quite naturally, this foolishness will be of value, and the old dream will be embodied, against the modern Prince, against politics as it exists concretely, and therefore against materialism and materialism alone. There is no problem of Marxism; there is only, once again, the problem of revolution.

This amounts to saying that the idea of an anti-Marxist politics is absurd, untenable, and a contradiction in terms. Anti-Marxism is and can be nothing but the contemporary form of the fight against politics. It also amounts to saying that for a long time to come, we are condemned to the language of *Capital* as long as we resign ourselves to playing the game of politics: Did the rebels of the Christian era have any other recourse against the secular rule of the Church than to appropriate the literal sense of the words of the gospels? Especially it amounts to saying that we will not go outside this language as we might leave an enclosure, that we will not be cured of this virus as we might recover from an illness. Like Ptolemaic cosmologists, we are confined within a closed space, without an outside or an elsewhere, and the weapons of criticism cannot tear down the barriers to point in the distance to the plains of felicity. We no longer have a politics, a language, or a recourse. There remain only ethics and moral duty. There remains only the duty to protest against Marxism, since we cannot forget it. And this is why I have so often spoken in imperatives.

Epilogue

Winter has done its work. A dark and faded sky hovers over the bare trees. A gloomy and frozen wind sweeps the world and turns it to stone. A wind from the East or a wind from the West? I have no idea, after all, for I have lost my compass and my charts. Socialism or capitalism? The question no longer means very much when the worst is possible. The slaves will live to be very old, dying without being able to die, dying from not dying, living their own death. The masters will be still older, and their fixed and murky eyes will survey the age and pour darkness down on men. When the wheels of history have been blocked and the promise has become a whisper, it remains for rats like us to find a corner in the ruins and wait there in peace. How sweet to live before the new barbarism! At this extreme point of the fate that will continue to dawn for a long time, there is a great temptation to make a bed out of fallen things, a heaven out of shattered dreams, and settle down to wait for irreparable wrong—surrender and abandonment before the procession of evil.

And then? Precisely then, we have to know how to say no. *No* to the temptation of warm surrender. *No* to abandonment and to the intoxication of saying "What's the good of it?" I have tried, indeed, to set down the foundations for what I have called "pessimism in history." I have struggled to track down to their final refuges the eternal dreams which govern the human herd. Perhaps I have even written a sad book, a very sad book, which, in these happy times, will seem the work of a dark and defeatist spirit, or of one who is weary of hoping. But is it necessary to be explicit? This project makes sense only if it is governed by an ethics which can be flatly called an ethics of *lucidity* and *truth*. Pessimism is of no value unless it brings forth at the end a slender but solid ground of *certainty* and *refusal*. In this strange game of living, in which our only remaining partner is the hidden approach of death, I say that we must give in less than ever before to the insupportable. I say that if we cannot raise him up, we must do everything in our power to prevent man from lowering himself.

Thus, if I were to go over one last time the path I have followed, encompass its method and its lessons in a single glance, and reduce it to the elements of a "practical philosophy," I would conclude like this: I have done nothing but raise in my way the three famous questions of the "Mandarin of Königsberg,"[1] nothing but tirelessly reiterate the arrogant challenges that he hurled at his century. *What can I know?* I have answered clearly, I hope: little, very little, except that the world is in a bad state, that its prophets of happiness are very often birds of doom, and that there is no worse danger today than disguise and deception. *What am I permitted to hope?* I have tried to answer with many arguments: little, very little, as well, if it is true that the Master is another name for the world, that as soon as one is dethroned another takes up the scepter, and that the red Princes are finally here, pawing at the threshold of power. *What, finally, should I do?* What is one permitted to will in these times of distress? I have said it along the way but I will repeat it in conclusion: We must hold high what Descartes called a "provisional morality," which for us can be summed up in this simple slogan: No matter where it may come from, resist the barbarian threat.

Resist from what standpoint? It goes without saying that never again will we be counselors to Princes, never again will we hold or strive for power. Plato knew this when, toward the end of his life, incredibly weary, he accepted the invitation of Dionysios of Syracuse: The adventure always turns out badly, and this is neither an appropriate role nor an appropriate place for a philosopher.[2] Cicero and Sallust learned it very quickly at their own expense: One does not "warn" Pompey with impunity, nor does one "enlighten" Caesar, for the price is sometimes the dignity and the very place of thought. The end of Diderot's dream, the reef on which it was wrecked, is well known: Catherine II restoring the use of the whip in the Russian countryside. We know what Voltairean enlightenment means: a sardonic alibi for Frederick's despotism. And we all remember the pitiful spectacle of a hallucinated Heidegger singing the praises of the Führer and the three "services" of the Reich. Philosophy has in fact held power at least twice in the West: in 1793 first, in the Committee of Public Safety, which held the Encyclopedia in one hand and the guillotine in the other; then in 1917, in the Marxist brains which, claiming to give birth to the good society, brought death to the world. The dream was not born yesterday, then, but it is established that it always turns into a blood bath.

With what weapons can we struggle? One thing more is certain: We will never again be guiding lights for the people; we will never again place ourselves at the "service" of the rebels. What do the "masses" need with the vain "principles" that intellectuals inoculate them with— a discreet reminder of millennial servitude? What does science matter to the rebels, since their whole history attests that they only enter into rebellion exactly in order *not to know,* to reject the order of time, its memory and its design? What good is our enlightenment to them, in the darkness of that *night* which they have made their home, once they have adopted the dream of breaking history in two?[3] In fact, the "revolutionary" intellectual is a pitiful figure—the salt of the earth, he thinks; in reality an executioner. The perennial "guides" speak a shameful and abject language, and they always, in the end, justify massacre and repression. Trotsky joined with the masses in 1917, he assassinated them in 1921. Lenin gave the land to the peasants in 1918, he took it back in 1919. The "mass line" in China was less the motive power of disorder on earth than the clamor of rediscovered order. There, too, the lesson is clear: We must, forever, give up "serving the people."

The way is indeed harsh and strait is the gate. If it is true that we are neither the bureaucrats nor the leaven of history, that the king doesn't give a damn for the wise man and that the wise man is not a king, that the masses

don't give a damn for enlightenment and that the enlightened abuse the masses, then this and simply this is left for
us: that we are that species which the West names Intellectuals, that we have to spell out that name and take on
that status, that it is urgent to accept it and to resign
ourselves to its misery. All that are left to us, against the
barbarian procession, are the weapons of our language
and the place on which we stand—the arms of our mu-
seums and the place of our solitude. We can testify about
the unspeakable and delay the horror, save what can be
saved and reject the intolerable. We will never again remake the world, but at least we can stay on guard to see
that it is not unmade. . . .

And this is why I claim that the antibarbarian intellectual will be first of all a metaphysician, and when I say
metaphysician I mean it in an angelic sense. To be sure,
we will no longer be *militants,* exiled as we are for a long
time to come from what is called politics. But the question
remains, and it is ours by right, of the *ontological* possibilities of the revolutionary event. No, we will no longer
carry men's *dreams* in our arms, for we know they are
futile and we are powerless. But the demand remains, and
it will be our concern, to make the maddest, most senseless of *wagers*: that it is possible to change man to his very
roots. Yes, we know that the world is subject to the law of
the Master, and we *do not believe* that that law will ever
give way to our desires. But we will continue *to think,* to
think to the end, *to think without believing it,* the impossible thought of a world freed from lordship. Why so? fools
will ask. Why persist in what has all the appearance of a
trap? Because it is from this place, and from this place

alone, from this "trap," as you call it, that it is at all possible to hunt down false appearances. And besides, without it, without its unreasonable demands, the world would be even worse than we say it is.

And this is why I claim that the antibarbarian intellectual will also be an artist. For art is nothing but the rampart built in every age against the emptiness of death, the chaos of shapelessness, and the quicksand of horror. For only the poet, the painter, and the musician know how to name evil and fish for its bloody pearls. For societies hardly have a choice in dealing with their surpluses— either perverse expenditure or sublime icons. For the artist, in a word, is the one who, out of necessity, has no ulterior motives, the one who, from the greatest disorder, can create the order of an image. I find it satisfying that my friend Marek Halter, who set out, mad with politics, to conquer kings, has returned, mad with despair,[4] to his canvas, the child of sorrow. I like the fact that André Malraux locked himself into his imaginary museum from the day he recognized man in the crouching creature "struggling against the earth" described in Les Noyers de l'Altenburg. I imagine that a people of poets would have been more capable than any other of resisting Nazism, that a shield of lights and shadows might have halted the river of mud. What is at stake is what psychoanalysts tell us sustains a cure: We must divert and condense, and thereby disarm, the evil spell of the death instinct. It is a question, in this illusion, of the future, neither more nor less, of civilization.

And this is why I claim that the antibarbarian intellectual, finally, will be a *moraliste*, and when I say *moraliste* I mean it in the classic sense, like Kant, Camus, or Mer-

leau-Ponty. I am fully aware of the secrets and the tricker-
ies of the categorical imperative, but I prefer that lie to
the lie of historicist superstition—a morality of courage
and duty confronting the dismal cowardice of submission
to facts. Of course I know that God has been dead since
Nietzsche, but I believe in the virtues of an atheist spiritu-
alism in the face of contemporary apathy and resignation
—something like an austere libertinism for a time of catastrophe. I don't believe in man either, and I am quite
willing to agree with my worthy teachers that he is in the
process of disappearing from the stage of thought; but I
simply believe that without a certain idea of man the
State soon surrenders to the whirlpool of fascism. I do not
grant the slightest theoretical value to what Marxists call
formal freedoms, but practically, here and now, I do not
see how we can deny their fabulous power to establish
and preserve the division of society, and consequently to
form a rampart against the barbarian temptation. In other
words, we are now in the disturbing position of having
nothing left with which to decide political questions but
the most fragile and uncertain tools. It is time, perhaps, to
write treatises on ethics.

Metaphysician, artist, *moraliste:* is all that enough to
make up what the tradition calls a rebel? Are we still
talking about what we call socialism? Nominalist to the
very end, I really believe that it is of the greatest urgency
that we bring ourselves to change the word.

Notes and References

PART ONE
THE SHEPHERD AND HIS FLOCK

1. I am well aware that for a Deleuzean there is no "material" economy that is not libidinal through and through, and vice versa. But when I speak of "materiality" I am pointing to something altogether different from what the weak Marxist argument does. I am pointing toward an opposition, which needs to be further elaborated and made more problematic, between *desire* and *suffering*.

2. I will often return to this notion of "naturalism." I am referring to the thesis according to which, beneath the layers of history, the sediment of institutions, or the "artifice" of the law, there remains some sort of good nature, still vital and in primeval form. "Beneath the paving stones, the beach . . ."

3. Étienne de La Boétie, *Discours de la servitude volontaire* (Paris: Payot, 1976).

4. On this point, I can do no better than refer to the great book by Guy Lardreau, *Le Singe d'or* (Paris: Mercure de France, 1973), about which it is not enough to say that it taught me to read Rousseau. And not the least of its virtues is to have discredited a certain number of readings, for example Derrida's (*De la grammatologie*, Paris: Éditions de Minuit, 1967).

PART TWO
ALL SORTS AND CONDITIONS OF MASTER

1. *L'Amour du censeur*, by Pierre Legendre, which was published in 1974 (Paris: Éditions du Seuil, "Le Champ freudien") is, to my knowledge, the first essay on Lacanian politics.

2. Oswald Spengler, *The Decline of the West* (New York: Alfred A. Knopf, 1928), vol. II, p. 184.

3. Jean-Claude Milner, "L'Amour de la langue," in nos. 6 and 7 of the Freudian periodical *Ornicar.*

4. I say "by force of circumstances" because it goes without saying that Leon Trotsky was *in reality* a pure product of Stalinism. And the quarrel of the thirties had to do with minor points which in no way interfered with the deep community of principles, and not only theoretical principles. On this point, see Kostas Mavrakis, who not long ago clarified matters (*Du Trotskysme*, Paris: Maspero, 1973).

5. Jean-Marie Benoist, "Héraclite et la Forêt-Noire," *Magazine littéraire*, September 1976.

6. I will sometimes have occasion in the course of this book to refer to Nietzsche, more precisely to Nietzsche's *politics.* I leave the question of his relationship to National Socialism open—it is not as simple as proponents of both sides of the argument believe. I also leave unresolved the delicate question of the dualism of wills, a question which I am not sure he raised clearly. I will simply point to the following, reserving an analysis in depth for later:

a. *the dual inheritance:* Nietzschians of the left and of the right, in the sense that one talks of left and right Hegelians;

b. *the critique of socialism,* whose principles seem to me thoroughly coherent, topical, and fruitful all at once.

7. Terminology borrowed from Georges Bataille, *Sur Nietzsche* (Paris: Gallimard, 1967).

8. See Pierre Nora et al., *Faire de l'histoire* (Paris: Gallimard, 1974), and especially Michel de Certeau, *L'Écriture de l'histoire* (Paris: Gallimard, 1975), whose arguments I am simply summarizing here.

9. See the fine analysis by Georges Poulet in *Études sur le temps humain* (Paris: Plon, 1950).

10. Pierre Clastres shows it clearly in *La Société contre l'État* (Paris: Éditions de Minuit, 1974), pp. 161–186.

11. *The Will to Power.*

12. Jean Hyppolite, *Introduction à la philosophie de l'Histoire de Hegel* (Paris: Marcel Rivière, 1947), p. 83.

13. This problem did not escape the attention of the authors of *L'Ange*. On this point, see the restatement by Christian Jambet in *L'Apologie de Platon* (Paris: Grasset, 1976), particularly his distinction between "barbaric" and "angelic" hatred of thought (p. 21).

PART THREE
THE TWILIGHT OF SOCIALISM

1. It would be ungracious not to recognize my debt here to François Fourquet, "L'Idéal historique," *Recherches*, 13, for in his essay there are some correct "views" on the question of socialism, which are by the way comically distinguished from Nietzschean rhetoric.

2. *Early Writings*, translated by Rodney Livingstone and Gregor Benton (New York: Vintage Books, 1975), p. 256.

3. G. Cottier, *L'Athéisme du jeune Marx* (Paris: Vrin, 1950). And Enrico de Negri, *La Teologia di Lutero, Rivelazione a Dialettica* (Florence, 1970).

4. Paris: Grasset, 1976.

5. Nikos Poulantzas, *Pouvoir politique et classes sociales* (Paris: Maspero, 1968), particularly II, 3; in English, *Political Power and Social Classes*, translation editor Timothy O'Hagan (London: NLB, 1975); *Les Classes sociales dans le capitalisme aujourd'hui* (Paris: Éditions du Seuil, 1974), pp. 16–28; in English, *Classes in Contemporary Capitalism*, translated by David Fernbach (London: NLB, 1975).

6. Louis Althusser, *Réponse à John Lewis* (Paris: Maspéro, 1973).

7. *The Dawn*, Section 206: "Phew! to believe that higher pay could abolish the *essence* of their misery—I mean their impersonal serfdom! Phew! to be talked into thinking that an increase in this impersonality, within the machinelike workings of a new society, could transform the shame of slavery into a virtue." *The Portable Nietzsche*, translated and edited by Walter Kaufmann (New York: The Viking Press, 1968), pp. 89–90.

8. Georges Bataille, on Stalin, in *La Souveraineté* (Paris: Gallimard, 1976).

9. *The Will to Power.*

10. *The Genealogy of Morals*, Third Essay, Section 8.

11. On this point see the analyses of Gilles Susong in *La Politique d'Orphée* (Paris: Grasset, 1974), particularly pp. 183 ff.

12. Michel Serres, *Hermès I* (Paris: Éditions de Minuit, 1969); article on Michel Foucault, 1964.

13. Plato, *Republic,* Book VII.

14. *Haine de la pensée* (Paris: Hallier, 1976), p. 54.

PART FOUR:
EVERYDAY FASCISM

1. *Voie d'accès au plaisir* (Paris: Grasset, 1974), pp. 17–27.

2. Guy Hocquenghem and René Schérer, "Coïre," *Recherches,* 19 (1976), p. 9.

3. Here is the passage in question: "Why do you, the political intellectuals, *feel for* the proletariat, out of compassion for what? I understand why a proletarian would hate you, not because you are bourgeois, privileged creatures with delicate hands, but because you do not dare to say the one thing it is important to say: that you can take sexual pleasure out of swallowing Capital's come, Capital's material productions, metal bars, polystyrene, books, sausages—swallowing tons of it until you burst. . . . Of course we suffer, we who are "capitalized," but that doesn't mean we don't have sexual pleasure, nor that what you think you can offer us—as a remedy for what, for what?—doesn't disgust us even more; we detest therapy and its vaseline, we prefer to stuff ourselves to death with the excesses you take to be the most stupid of all. And don't expect our spontaneity to rebel either." *Économie libidinale* (Paris: Éditions de Minuit, 1974), pp. 141–142.

4. Félix Guattari, *Psychanalyse et politique* (Paris: Éditions du Seuil, 1974), pp. 43–60. Contrast the beautiful essays by Sollers and J.-J. Goux.

5. On this point, I must indicate a deep disagreement with Christian Jambet and Guy Lardreau, for whom, whatever the social effects of Deleuzism, Deleuze is and remains a great philosopher who can in no way be reduced to those effects. See Jambet's homage to Deleuze in a note to *L'Apologie de Platon.*

6. I want to pay tribute here to a man forgotten by fashion, a semi-outlaw of modernity, Kostas Axelos, the author of *Marx, penseur de la technique* (reprinted, Paris: U.G.E. 10/18, 1974), to whom, on this particular point, I owe a great deal.

7. *Des Dispositifs pulsionnels* (Paris: U.G.E. 10/18, 1974), p. 17.

8. See once again *L'Apologie de Platon* by Jambet, pp. 115–119.

9. No doubt, on this point as on many others, there has been a perceptible shift in Foucault's latest works. I mean *Surveiller et punir* and especially *La Volonté de savoir,* where the concept of "productive

power" makes its appearance while that of "rarefaction," which had been central until then, vanishes.

10. Michel Foucault was kind enough to explain himself on this in an interview with me published by *Le Nouvel Observateur,* March 14, 1977.

11. Auguste Comte, *Cours de philosophie positive,* 56ᵉ leçon (Paris: Herman, 1975). "Monotheism" is defined there as the aspiration to "actively direct mental movement."

12. *Group Psychology and the Analysis of the Ego,* translated and edited by James Strachey (New York: Norton, 1959), p. 13.

13. Freud, *Civilization and Its Discontents.*

14. Guy Coquille, *Institution du droit des Français* (1605); Charles Loyseau, *Traité des seigneuries* (1613). Both plagiarize or comment on *Six livres de la République* by Jean Bodin (1576).

15. Étienne Pasquier, *Les Recherches de la France:* Kings, "out of natural benevolence toward their subjects, reducing their absolute power under the civility of the law, obey their commands."

16. "Statutory decrees" constituted a kind of supplementary law filling in the gaps in the king's decrees, and "judgments of equity" an easing or extension of the law according to the character of the trial in progress.

17. Achille de Harlay, first president of the Parlement de Paris.

18. See the very important article by Marcel Gauchet, "L'Expérience totalitaire et la pensée de la politique," *Esprit,* July–August 1976, pp. 20–21.

PART FIVE:
THE NEW PRINCE

1. André Glucksmann deserves recognition for being the first to take this into account. Hence, among other reasons, the "crucial" character of his *La Cuisinière et le mangeur d'hommes* (Paris: Éditions du Seuil, 1975).

2. "Work is a matter of honor, a matter of glory, a matter of courage and heroism."

3. See Françoise Paul-Lévy, *Karl Marx, histoire d'un bourgeois allemand* (Paris: Grasset, 1976), demonstrating that all this was already in the canonic texts or in their margins.

4. This is why an analysis of Soviet society in the manner of Foucault is necessary today. Glucksmann attempted it in *La Cuisinière* and he clearly showed how the schemata of Western "enclosure"

were valid for the institution of the camp. This work will one day have to be pursued, and it will be necessary to show how this same camp represents the edge, the boundary, the outside through which the Soviet "inside" takes on form and substance.

5. See the book by Claude Lefort, *Un Homme en trop* (Paris: Éditions du Seuil, 1976), again about Solzhenitsyn, to which I owe a great deal. And in passing I would like to pay tribute to the effort undertaken around the periodical *Textures* to analyze the mechanisms of Soviet society. See for example the essay by Castoriadis in number 12: "Valeur, égalité, justice, politique: de Marx à Aristote et d'Aristote à nous." Reprinted in *Les Carrefours du labyrinthe* (Paris: Editions du seuil, 1978), pp. 249–316.

6. See J.-M. Palmier, *Les Écrits politiques de Heidegger* (Paris: L'Herne). "Total mobilization, as the ultimate stage of metaphysics, designates the taking charge of the fate of the West and of the entire World by the figure of the worker."

7. Ernst Niekrisch, German socialist, who later became a Marxist.

8. Herman Rauschnig, one of the first National Socialists, a member of the party as early as 1931, a convinced nationalist, rebelled against the Führer and was exiled to America, where he died.

9. *The Will to Power.*

10. *La Souveraineté* (Paris: Gallimard, 1976).

11. *Change,* 2, May 1969.

12. In German: *"Rohen und gedankenlosen Kommunismus."*

13. See the mechanics of the "plan for reconstruction" by J. P. Fourcade in the fall of 1974.

14. See my article "Pour un nouveau modèle de croissance," published in the first issue of *La Nouvelle Revue socialiste.*

15. Among others, Pierre Bruno (with C. Clément and L. Sève), *Pour une Critique marxiste de la théorie psychanalytique* (Paris: Éditions Sociales).

16. Pierre Macherey, *Pour une Théorie de la production littéraire* (Paris: Maspero, 1966).

17. *Une Crise et son enjeu* (Paris: Maspero, 1973), which attempts to state clearly the principles of a "materialist epistemology," and *Lyssenko* (Paris: Maspero, 1976), which attempts a "materialist treatment" of the famous "affair."

18. For numismatics, see Suzanne de Brunhoff, *La Monnaie chez Marx* (Paris: Éditions Sociales). For urbanism, François Ascher, *Demain la ville* (Paris: Éditions Sociales). And for the rest, the whole catalogue of Éditions Sociales.

19. Daniel Lindenberg, *Le Marxisme introuvable* (Paris: Calmann-Lévy, 1975).

20. A concept created by Gramsci but adopted by contemporary communist ideologues.

21. Valéry Giscard d'Estaing, *Démocratie française* (Paris: Fayard, 1976).

22. Argan: "We must preserve the sacred character of Rome."

23. There would be a good deal to say about the function of Garaudy and Garaudism in the socialist heaven and hell. Foil? Negative alibi? Scapegoat? No end is in sight, in any case, of charging him with the totality of deviationist sins.

24. I emphasize, for the sake of historical truth, that I myself was never directly involved in the Maoist adventure, but that I held it to be, and still do today, one of the very great pages of the recent history of France.

25. I am thinking here especially of Maurice Clavel. It is impossible to overemphasize the fact that *because he is a Christian,* he is capable of historically accurate judgment; with the reservation of some disagreements of detail which I think he knows quite well.

26. We need a debate about fundamentals, which I have neither the space nor the means to undertake here. This is all the more true because *La Volonté de savoir,* published after these lines were written, considerably enriches Foucault's problematics on this point. Foucault, then, more than ever the "educator."

27. Particularly Engels's *The Peasant War in Germany.*

EPILOGUE

1. Nietzsche, in *The Will to Power,* referring to Kant.

2. Having said this, it should be recalled that Jambet has shown that the Platonic *dream* was never that of the "Counselor of the Prince," but, and this is altogether different, the dream of a Master who would no longer be a Master, who would abolish the principle of all lordship, and whom he names, *for lack of a better term,* "philosopher-king." The Syracuse adventure should thus be understood as a solution chosen out of *despair,* and not as the mirage of some intellectual and moral reform of the *polis.*

3. Jambet and Lardreau again, in a conversation with Gilles Hertzog published in *Magazine littéraire,* July 1976.

4. An exemplary journey recorded in *Le Fou et les Rois* (Paris: Albin Michel, 1976).

Index